Gene Jelks

Walking Across the Bridge

His Story, His Journey & His Restoration

2016

Rapier
PUBLISHING COMPANY

Scripture verses depicting KJV, or not marked are taken from the Spirit-Filled Bible, King James Version, Copyright © 1991, 1995 by Thomas Nelson, Inc. All rights reserved.

Scripture verses depicting the NLT are taken from the Holy Bible, The New Living Translation, Copyright © 1996, 2004, Tyndale House Publishers Inc., Wheaton, IL 60189, USA. All rights reserved.

Walking Across the Bridge
His Story, His Journey & His Restoration

Copyright © 2016 by Gene Jelks

ISBN 978-09966083-9-8
Library of Congress Control Number 2015957379

Published by
Rapier Publishing Company
260 W. Main Street, Suite #1
Dothan, Alabama 36301
www.rapierpublishing.com

Printed in the United States of America
All rights reserved under the International Copyright Law. Contents and/or cover may not be reproduced in whole or in part in any form without the consent of the Publisher or Author.

Book Cover Design: Garrett Myers/ Book Layout: Rapture Graphics
Editor Cathy Ledbetter

Cover Pictures: all reprinted with permission. All Rights Reserved.
Front Cover: Gene in Suit. Photo by Lisa Tisdale © Reprinted with permission.
Front Cover: Gene running with Ball. © Courtesy of Tuscaloosa News. "Era of Mediocrity Followed Alabama's 1992 Title, dtd. 12/23/12. Tommy Deas/ tommy@tidesports.com
Back Cover: Gene With Children. © Courtesy of AL.com. Article: "GENE JELKS FOOTBALL CAMP &-12-14." dtd. 7/12/14. Joe Songer/Jsonger@Al.com ©

The views expressed in this work are solely those of the author and do not necessarily reflect the views of the publisher, and the publisher hereby disclaims any responsibility for them.

Dedication

I dedicate this book to my Lord and Savior, Jesus Christ.

To my mother, Doris A. Jelks, my father, the late Daniel A. Jelks, my sister, Audry L. Jelks, and my brothers, Reverend Anthony C. Jelks, and Danté L. Jelks

I love you guys with all my heart. You have encouraged me with your love and support. You never gave up on me and pushed me to overcome my struggles.

Thank You!

Foreword

I first met Gene Jelks thirty years ago, back when I was a coach at the University of Alabama. I recruited him as a high school football player to play for Alabama. He was a young man of great character and enormous athletic talent. Since the time I first met him as a promising high school player up until now, Gene has endured many things, and like most of us, some of those things he endured took him to places he didn't dream of going. However, like the "gifted" athlete he is and has demonstrated on the field, Gene was, and still is, a fighter, never giving up, overcoming all the opponents and obstacles that challenged him. He endured to the end zone and scored the touchdown. In the end, he found the source that he was searching for, and that source was God. It was in this Source, that Gene was able to come out of the tackle unblemished and ready to play again; yet, this time, for a team that never loses.

Today, Gene is at a different place in his life than when he started out as a young man playing football in high school, and later at Alabama. He is at a place right now where he is content and happier than he has ever been before. He is utilizing his football skills, talents and life experiences as a coach to help and nurture young people. He is spending his time and resources to be a positive influence and role model for the next generation. I am thankful that I had a small role to play in his life and journey, and I am very happy for him and the place he's matured to in his life. For Gene now understands that sometimes in life you have to first go under the bridge to walk across the bridge.

~Coach Ray Perkins~
Former Alabama Head Coach, 1983-1986

Acknowledgments

Gene Jelks and I have been friends since childhood. I have had the esteemed pleasure of spending time with Gene not only on the field but also as a friend. It is widely known that Gene is a very gifted athlete, who has experienced success on every level of the game of football. He is one of the most gifted athletes that I have ever had the pleasure of lining up against.

I am grateful to have witnessed firsthand how God orchestrated Gene's life from the very beginning until now. Gene and I stayed in touch until his departure from the University of Alabama. After his professional football career ended, Gene went underground for decades. I reached out to him, visited his mom, and constantly tried to locate him to no avail. Then one day Gene called me. He shared with me all that he had gone through over the last twenty years, without any reservations. I let Gene finish telling me his story, realizing he needed to vent. After hearing his story, I realized that even though he had lost all he had, he had not lost his faith in God.

After hearing Gene's heart, I said to Gene, "It's time to come home." I told him, "You've been gone away from people who love you far too long. There are more people in Alabama who love you than there are against you." I invited Gene to speak at New Destiny Church. I knew there was a divine purpose for all that had taken place in his life. I quickly realized that God was ready to use Gene's story to bring himself Glory. God has now brought Gene "Across the Bridge". He has healed Gene from the hurt of his past and has reconciled his broken relationships. I am so proud to see what God is doing in Gene's life. I pray that his book blesses your life, as he shares his heart with the world. I am glad to say that I am a friend of Gene Jelks. I am convinced that the best is yet to come. Gene is a super guy and one of the best people you can ever meet. I am thankful for our lifelong friendship.

-Steve Smith Sr.-
Senior Pastor
New Destiny Christian Church
Gadsden, Alabama

As a pastor and as Gene's brother, I always tell him to forget all those things from his past, especially the ones that caused pain and turmoil. Always go back and reflect to see where He, Jesus, has brought you from but don't go back. Learn from your mistakes, and glean the lessons from your past, but don't go back and allow your past to dictate your present and your future. There's a reason why it's called the past. The same goes for anyone. If you linger in the past, you will never get to where you want and need to go.

I'm proud of my brother, and where the Lord is leading him. His journey walking across the bridge had some rough spots, and many obstacles and hurdles, but now, he is at the end of the bridge, and learning that the fullness of Christ determines what is ahead of you, not behind you. For Gene has learned and is still learning what Paul was referring to when he wrote these profound words:

"Though I might also have confidence in the flesh. If any other man thinketh that he hath whereof he might trust in the flesh, I more: Circumcised the eighth day, of the stock of Israel, of the tribe of Benjamin, an Hebrew of the Hebrews; as touching the law, a Pharisee; Concerning zeal, persecuting the church; touching the righteousness which is in the law, blameless. But what things were gain to me, those I counted loss for Christ. Yea doubtless, and I count all things but loss for the excellency of the knowledge of Christ Jesus my Lord: for whom I have suffered the loss of all things, and do count them but dung, that I may win Christ, And be found in him, not having mine own righteousness, which is of the law, but that which is through the faith of Christ, the righteousness which is of God by faith: That I may know him, and the power of his resurrection, and the fellowship of his sufferings, being made conformable unto his death; If by any means I might attain unto the resurrection of the dead. Not as though I had already attained, either were already perfect: but I follow after, if that I may apprehend that for which also I am apprehend

ed of Christ Jesus. Brethren, I count not myself to have apprehended: but this one thing I do, forgetting those things which are behind, and reaching forth unto those things which are before, I press toward the mark for the prize of the high calling of God in Christ Jesus." Philippians 3:4-14 (KJV)

~Reverend Anthony C. Jelks~
Pastor/Brother

Table of Contents

Introduction

The Foot of the Bridge (The Starting Point)..........17
   1. The Journey Begins..........17
   2. The Gift..........31
   3. Roll Tide..........45
   4. Sweet Home Alabama..........55
   5. From Offense to Defense..........63

At the Crossroad (The Middle of the Bridge)..........71
   6. When the Crowd Stopped Cheering..........71
   7. First Comes Pride, Then the Fall..........85
   8. Under the Bridge..........95
   9. The Prodigal Son Returns..........105
   10. Going Home..........113

The Long Walk Home (The End of the Bridge)..........121
   11. Grace Restored..........121
   12. Forgiveness is Not an Option..........131
   13. The Road to Restoration..........139
   14. Giving Back..........147
   15. It Was All in God's Plan..........155

Introduction

I have been gone for over twenty years, hidden and cast aside like an abandoned building once full of light and glory, now fallen and ready to crumble with the first strong wind. Through it all, I have seen the good, the not so good, and the downright ugly. I experienced joy, and I experienced pain. I must admit, if it weren't for the grace of God, the pain would've killed me. In my 50 years, I have done some walking. I have walked in the valley, by the river, in the mud, and in the water. I walked in the rain, snow, and sleet. I have even walked among the flowers. Many people ask me why I need to tell my story. I need to tell my story because I never really had a chance to tell my story from this point of view: The Truth. The truth sometimes has an ugly way of revealing things to you and to others that no one wants to see. The truth will expose us even when we are trying our best to cover up our issues, our flaws, and our shortcomings. There are facts, and then there is the truth. The facts show the perceived truth, but the truth shows the reality behind the facts. The truth shows what really took place.

At the end of your life, after the funeral, after the tears, after you have been laid to rest, the only thing people will see is your tombstone on your grave. Three significant things are on a tombstone: The day you were born, the day you died, and your name. Everything between your date of birth and the date of your death reflects your name; what you did on this earth while you were here. I don't want people to remember me as a could-have-been, a should-have-been, or a has-been for that matter. I want people to remember me as a man who, in the midst of adversity, in the midst of a crisis, did the right thing. I want people to remember me as a man who allowed God to heal, deliver and transform him into what he was called to be…a person who lived up to his name. The name he got from his father.
You may be wondering, but why now? As I have said many times,

time heals all wounds. Sometimes we have to go deep in the barrel, the bottom of the tar pit, before we cry out and say, "Help!" It's in this place, in the darkness of night, where we start to see the light. It's in this place where we start to see the truth. Because when everyone is cheering for us and calling our name, when we are at the "top of our game," that's when the vision can get blurred, and we can't see clearly. When people want to say, "I know him," and everyone wants to shake our hand and be our friend, we can't see anything because the crowd is huge. But when the cheering stops, and we are on the other side of the fence and darkness comes like a thief in the night, that's when we begin to see.

I was at the foot of the bridge about to walk across it, not understanding how both ends, though they look alike, were so different. One is the starting point, the other, the ending point. What we fail to realize is that in between the points, the start, and the finish, is where we are actually walking across the bridge to get to our destination. And that's where I had to start my story, the starting point, or the beginning of the bridge, in order for me to walk across it.

A bridge is defined as a structure that's built to span physical obstacles such as a body of water, valley or road, for the purpose of providing safe passage over the obstacles. The bridge that I had to walk across, and am still walking across, also had many obstacles along the way. Some paths I took I wish I hadn't taken, but thank God for His grace. It was only His grace that got me back on the right path.

So here is my story. The funny thing about my story, is that it's your story too. The main differences are the players and the scenario, but when you read it, I'm quite sure you will see yourself in it too. However, the major difference between my story and your story is that you may not have been in the "spotlight". No one may have known about your struggles or your hasty decisions; whereas, many people knew all about mine. In your story, you may not have been publicly judged, and didn't have to deal openly with your consequences as I did, but in the end, you still had to walk across your bridge. Whether we are star athletes, professional, career-minded people, movie stars, pop singers, or everyday individuals, we all have to walk across the bridge.

I pray that as you read this book, my story, it will inspire you to see the bridges in your life from a different perspective. I pray that God will deliver you, heal you, and show you, as you walk across the bridge to get to your destination.

-Eugene Jelks-

The Foot of the Bridge
(The Starting Point)

Chapter 1
The Journey Begins

I was born on January 21, 1966, in a small southern town called Gadsden in the state of Alabama. It was a pivotal time in the history of our country to be born. Our country was at unrest on two fronts. On the national level, the Civil Rights Movement was in full swing, and internationally, the Vietnam War was still raging in Southeast Asia. I was the oldest of four children. It was me, my sister Audry, my brother Anthony and my baby brother Dante'. My father, Daniel A. Jelks, was a skilled construction worker and plumber. He worked at the Republic Steel Plant in Gadsden as a foreman. At that time, such a position was rarely given to a black man, but my father was no ordinary man. He was a smart and hard-working man, who was very protective of his family. He loved his wife and kids. His favorite pastime was gardening. He would stay in his garden for hours at a time. He taught us family values, to have respect for each other, to communicate if we have a problem, not to be selfish and most importantly, to love Jesus. Even though he wasn't as spiritual as my mother, he loved Jesus. I remember my dad taking us to his small family church in Rock Spring, Alabama every time they held a revival to hear his former preacher, Reverend Terry, preach. He was a preaching machine! I don't know if people came for the revival, or just to hear Reverend Terry's charismatic preaching, but there was always a full house and standing room only in the church, out to the church door. During those revivals, the Holy Ghost permeated the atmosphere!

My father led by example. He had a strong work ethic, and he always provided and took care his family. He didn't like handouts. One thing I loved about my father was his wonderful sense of humor. He would always say something to make our family and others laugh or smile. He may not have been one of the Kings of Comedy, but in a different time and place, he could've been a renowned comedian. He loved sports too, especially baseball. He was a great baseball catcher; in fact, in my opinion, he was the best in Gadsden. For these reasons and many more, my dad was a great part of my accomplishments, on and off the football field. He was always there for my siblings and me. Having a man like my dad in my life to affirm me was very important to me. Every son needs a dad to affirm him. I am just thankful that I had that type of dad. Sadly, when my father died in 1994 of cancer, it would change the dynamics of our family and my life forever. I felt alone and lost. I knew he was going to be with the Lord, but on the day he died, I lost my best friend. I cried many tears for many years until God healed me and gave me peace about his death.

My mother, Doris A. Jelks, worked at Goodyear Tire and Rubber Company as a tire builder. She was raised in the church. And boy, could my mother sing and play the piano! She loved her husband and family very much. She taught us the value of family togetherness by doing almost everything together, such as going to church and Sunday School, playing games, watching television together, and visiting her side of the family, or, as we called it, traveling to the country. Most importantly, she taught us to love people and always trust, believe and follow Jesus.

To help my father make ends meet, on the weekends, she worked as a cook in a restaurant called "The Royal Palm." She also played the piano at the First Baptist Church in Alabama City. That's what family did back then. When my mother was in the kitchen cooking dinner, I was outside playing football or playing hide and seek. Back then, children were not allowed to play in the kitchen or be in the kitchen when grownups were cooking. I was allowed in the kitchen when she baked a cake. I would wait until she emptied the batter from the bowl; then I'd run my finger around it and lick what was left of the sweet cake mix until the bowl was clean. Those were the only times I was allowed in the kitchen. My mother was sweet, but she didn't play. My parents had rules, and we had better follow them, or else. My mother gave us all chores to do. I was the oldest, so I had to make sure the rest of my siblings did their chores.

As the overseer of my siblings, it was my job to make sure they had done their homework and housework before my parents came home from work. After we had come home from school, we had to take off our school clothes and put on our play clothes and get busy with our chores and homework. When my mother came home and saw that everything was done, she would then let us go outside and play with the neighbor's kids until sundown. After supper, it was bath time and off to bed. My mother always had a set bedtime for us, which was around 10 p.m. I couldn't wait until the week was over because we were allowed to stay up later on the weekend. Back then, children were children and parents were parents. They were not our friends. It's so much different today. Times were simpler then than they are now.

We didn't have a lot of material things growing up, but we had everything we needed. We always had plenty of food to eat and clean clothes to wear. My parents always provided a good home for us. My brother and I shared a bedroom with twin beds. My sister had her own bedroom. Later, when God blessed our family with another baby brother, the room situation changed. I especially liked the holidays because we would get new clothes and new shoes. Also, during the Christmas holidays, my parents would drive us around the neighborhood to see all the beautifully decorated homes. We enjoyed sight-seeing and just being together with family. My family on both sides was close-knit, and we loved each other. We are still that way today. One of the greatest feelings in the world is being loved by your family.

The black families in our neighborhood were close and looked out for each other. Going to church and school were the main activities for both the youth and the adults. Living in Gadsden, Alabama was no different than living in any other small city in the South. Gadsden is a blue-collar town of working citizens with lots of low-paying jobs. Gadsden is located in Northeast Alabama between Birmingham, Alabama and Chattanooga, Tennessee. It borders along the Coosa River and near the main part of the Appalachian Ridge. It has two hospitals, Gadsden Regional and Riverview Regional Medical Center. In 2014, the population was 36,888, and the median cost of a house was $70,000. It's 20.40% lower in cost of living than the national average in the United States. The city used to be one of the state's largest industrial centers, right behind Mobile. When I was growing up, Gadsden's major productions were steel, rubber, fabricated metal and electronic equipment. The most prominent factories were Goodyear Tire and Rubber Company and Republic Steel Corporation. The steel plant, as the city folks called it, later became Gulf States Steel. It closed completely down in the year 2000, leaving behind barren landscapes and many workers out of a job. There were not many jobs in the town, which left the economic situation grim, and as a result, many people left and moved up north or out west to find work.

Gadsden is called the "The City of Champions," but during that time, we looked like anything but champions. Schools were segregated, and railroad tracks divided the community. When the steel plant closed and the tire and rubber plant partially closed (it eventually came back full force), opportunities for advancement were slim to none for all people, both black and white and so our family was all that we had. I was fortunate because I had both of my parents in my life along with my sister and two little brothers. My parents worked hard at physically strenuous jobs to provide for us.

My family is known in the town as being good Christian folks. My mother had a renowned world-class singing voice. She took us to church every Sunday, and we attended Sunday school. We attended First Baptist Church in Alabama City, but my Aunt Paulette attended Shiloh Missionary Baptist Church in Gadsden. My mother would send us to Sunday school there and then she would take us to our church afterward. Our family prayed together all the time. I remember after church every Sunday, the women in the family would cook a feast of soul food, with big pitchers of cold Lipton ice tea and flavored Kool-Aid. To top it off, we had delicious homemade cakes. We would all sit down and eat Sunday dinner together. In the summer time, we would get out the ice cream freezers and make our own ice cream. It was right out of a movie, but that's how most families lived back then.

On some Sundays and holidays, my parents would drive us to my dad's family's home to visit our grandmother. I never knew my paternal grandfather. He died before I got to know him. My uncle told me that he was a medical doctor, but was never looked upon as a doctor regardless of his medical degree. The white folks would only call him when a member of their family was too sick to go to the doctor, or if they couldn't pay for a white doctor. He never received his just due as a medical doctor. I was blessed to have been able to know my grandmother. It was so much fun visiting her because she had chickens and goats. I remember chasing her chickens until they ran under her house.

My maternal grandmother, lived in Alabama City, Alabama right outside of Gadsden. My maternal grandfather, Y.Z. Mostiller, my mother's father, died at the age of 42 of a heart attack. I never got to know him either. My aunt told me later that he was waiting for me to be born when he had the heart attack and died. She said that he was a hard-working, blue-collar worker at the steel plant where he was the first black train conductor in Alabama City. My grandmother would be the one to hold the family together and provide for her children when her husband died. Like most of the women on both sides of our family, she was a great cook. We called her "Mudear", but her Christian name was Christene Gary Madien. Mudear and her children lived in a small community close to the steel plant. Times were so tough, they all shared a bedroom. My mother used to tell us how she remembers taking turns to bathe on the back porch in an aluminum tub.

Sometimes as a special treat, my sister and I would get to spend the weekend with our grandparents, and boy, that was fun! We would get to ride to the store with them, and they would buy us toys, take us to visit our other relatives, take us to church on Sundays, and give us money. I loved my grandmother's Sunday dinners. She was a great cook. Of course, we were closer to our relatives than to anyone else in the community, and though my mother had many friends that we visited from time to time, being with family was a priority.

My parents always told us that we were special and that God had something extraordinary for each of us. So while still just a boy, this gave me the confidence to start a car washing business. Every summer, my uncles would come down from up north; they became my regular customers. As a side business, I sold pecans that I had gathered from my grandmother's pecan trees that grew in her yard. I picked up the nuts from sun up to sundown, then bagged them up and sold them from the table I had set up in our community. If I had any bags left toward the end of the day, I marked down the price for a quick sale. With my parents encouraging my industrious nature, I was not afraid to work hard to pursue success even then. It was no surprise to them that I was a born entrepreneur.

It was this kind of diligence that drove me to discover my love for football. I would become addicted to football at the age five. In the first grade I went to a Catholic school where I was an altar boy. Each day during the Physical Education, my classmates and I would play football, and even though I was the smallest boy on the field, I began to love the thrill of the game. I loved running with the football and being the first one to get to the end zone. We would play on an open 50-yard grass field. The older boys would give me the football and block for me, and I would run and score a touchdown. They told me I was lightning fast. At my private school, we didn't have a real football team, so I watched the public schools' football teams. I told my parents I wanted to go to public school so I could play organized football. My mother allowed my sister, brother and I to attend public school the next year. From then on, I played football. I played pee-wee, junior high and high school football. I played in my yard or the neighbor's yard, wherever there was a place to play, I played. It became my dream even then as a little boy to play for The University of Alabama because all I heard growing up was the name Bear Bryant. Coach Paul "Bear" Bryant, the head coach at Alabama was a household name. And after I played for him, my next goal was to become a professional football player in the National Football League. Because I knew I was born to run.

Up until I was ten, and in the fifth grade, I went to an all-black school called Carver Elementary. After that, the schools were integrated. The first years of integration were some scary times for the blacks in our area and for me too as a young boy. I witnessed the Ku Klux Klan holding rallies in my town as a little boy. I didn't understand why they wore white robes and hoods that looked like cones at the top. My mother taught us to love everybody regardless of what we saw or felt. When the KKK held their rallies, my mother told us to stay in the yard and to continue to play. We did. However, even as a little boy, I felt confused and sad, because they did a lot of bad things to black people and called us the "N" word. We were just innocent children playing. I remember there was a corner store in our neighborhood. A man named Mr. Buck would sell food to the blacks and allow them to get things on credit if they didn't have any money. He had a grandson who worked with him. When I would go to the store with my family, I would have to say "yes sir" to his grandson, even though he was seven years old, the same age as me. This was confusing to me as an impressionable young boy.

It was in those crazy times of civil unrest that football became my escape. I would go to bed with a football and get up with a football. On the weekends in my neighborhood, I would always carry it around in my hands. I would play street football with my cousins and friends. I always had bruises and scrapes on my hands and knees from playing football. When I got pushed down by the other boys, I kept going. I would get up and try again. This made me get tougher because all the other boys were older and bigger. I learned to ignore the bumps and the bruises. After the football games, my friends and I would steal some plums in my neighbor's backyard. One day the neighbor spotted us climbing his fence, and he got his gun out and fired one shot into the air. We scattered like pigeons. He told our parents, and all of us got the beating of our lives. Needless to say, I never did that again. (My mother is a sweet, loving woman, but she doesn't play!)

I can honestly say I had a wonderful childhood growing up. It was, for the most part, idyllic; however, most people at some point in their lives will have a dark moment or event that they wish they could erase from their mind. Mine, unfortunately, happened when I was very young. When these things happen, it's difficult, if not impossible, to ever forget, and most of the time, it can leave damaging scars that can haunt a person forever. Even though it's difficult to understand, with time, it loses some of its hold, yet it still leaves its impact. My darkest moment came at the age of five when I was molested by a neighbor. He sexually abused me; then he told me not to tell anyone, or he would kill me, and also my family. I was physically and mentally frightened. I feared for my life and for my family's lives, so I kept it inside. I would come to relive this scene of the man molesting me over and over. This horror replayed itself inside my head to the point that I would get depressed and sometimes angry. The molestation incident caused me to feel emotional pain and psychological trauma. Up until then, I'd never encountered that kind of torment before in my young life. I was a good boy who didn't like trouble. I asked God, "Why did this have to happen to me?" My parents reared disciplined kids; we were no thugs. Thankfully, even though this unfortunate event happened, it didn't kill or stop me from pursuing my goals. I learned to suppress and cope with it, in spite of the scar it left on me. It wasn't until last year, in February 2015, on a Sunday afternoon, that I finally felt the release and peace in my heart to tell my family about that incident. I built up the courage to gather my family together and I told them what happened that day in the woods. It was a shock to my family, and they were devastated, but God got us through it. In hindsight, I would learn as I walked across the bridge, this incident caused me more damage than I realized.

In my youth, I rarely got into fights, but when the older boys in the neighborhood picked on me, I did fight them back. Sometimes I would win and sometimes I would lose. My fights with those boys made me feel alone because I didn't have a big brother to protect me, as some of them did. My mother taught us to behave and be nice to people. That's why I avoided trouble. Besides, I didn't like to get into trouble because if the neighbors heard or saw me do something wrong, my mother and grandmother gave them permission to whip my butt and then when they came home from work they would whip my butt too. That was called double trouble! (Back then, that's how it was for most kids.)

Gene Jelks

I remember joining the Boys and Girls Club of Gadsden when I was nine years old. My older cousin Tony would walk with me to the club. At the club, I played basketball, softball and other sports and activities. The club helped me learn teamwork and esprit de corps. It also built up my confidence and my self-esteem because the counselors were good people who cared about us. They always encouraged us to do well in life and stay out of trouble. Those teachings would stick with me as I was growing up. I applied the lessons from my Christian background, along with the tools I had learned at the club toward my life at school and on the football field.

We didn't have a lot of toys growing up, and that's why it was a special treat for us to visit our grandparents. My friends and I would create different kinds of games to entertain ourselves in the neighborhood. We often played marbles, which was a popular pastime back then. We never considered ourselves poor; we just enjoyed what we had and tried to have fun and be happy no matter what the situation. Besides, everyone was in the same boat as we were.

Every summer I attended Vacation Bible School at our family church. I recall one memorable day when the pastor gave the invitation to accept Jesus; something drew me to Him as my Lord and Savior. My church had always had an impact on me, so that day I accepted Jesus as my Savior. I was 13 years old. After that, my walk with Jesus helped me cope with the emotional aspect of being molested. It helped me to put it in the back of my mind and concentrate more on other things instead, such as running with my football. It had been a heavy burden carrying the memories of that incident, and it left a scar. I still have this scar on my heart, but it didn't have as much of an effect on me then because I was playing football at school and football took my mind off it most of the time. And this was crucial so I could focus on my dream, which was football.

We didn't have a lot of entertainment growing up. It was church, Vacation Bible School and every once in a while my mother would let us go to the skating rink on Sunday nights. I had a lot of fun skating and talking to the girls, but if we didn't go to church, my mother wouldn't allow us to go to the skating rink. She didn't play about the things concerning the Lord. Sometimes she would let me walk to my aunt's house and walk back home. As I got older, my mother would let me walk to my cousin Jerry's apartment complex. We would sit out on his steps and talk. He would listen to me tell him about my football games when I was in the ninth grade as a freshman running back. I always looked forward to talking with big "Cuz" about football and other things young boys talk about.

Football not only became my outlet, but it also became my life. Playing peewee football was when I became a running back. The quarterback would hand me the ball and the line would block the defenders. I would find a hole in the line and run as fast as I could toward the goal line without letting a defensive player tackle me. When I scored my first touchdown, something took off inside me. Football would be the beginning of my new life. Life was good for me, especially on days when I would score five touchdowns in a game. Many people would say, "That little boy is incredibly fast." When I lined up against the defense and got the ball, I outran all eleven of the opponent's players. I had to because football is a harsh, physical sport and I didn't like to get hit, especially since the defensive boys were so much bigger than me.

At that age, I was just discovering my gift; that gift was the gift of speed. I spent most of my time developing my skill and talent as a running back. I still had to go to church or else my mother wouldn't let me play football. As I said, I believe I used football as an escape to help me get my mind off the horror of being molested. Football helped me to block the pain and gave me some relief from the tormenting memories and the threats from the neighbor. It was a relief and gave me peace of mind if I dwelled on football instead of that incident. My coach in peewee football, Coach Ragland, told me that I was too little and too skinny, but he gave me the football anyway. I would do all the drills just like the bigger boys. When I played on defense, no one on our team could catch or tackle the opponents the way I could. I would outrun them all. My coach said the bigger kids couldn't catch me and that I had exceptional skills and talent as a running back. Sometimes he would even sit me on the bench because I ran too many touchdowns in a game. He said I was ahead of my time and a cut above the rest. At one time, he thought the other teams were not that good, but he called me an amazing football player. (I believed he said those things to keep me from getting a "Big Head.")

I attended General Forrest Middle School. The school was integrated now, having enrolled both black and white students. It took some time to get use to attending school with whites. I played in the band, and I played football. I would have to ask the band teacher, Ms. Turner if I could leave band practice early so I could go to football practice. She always allowed me to go. One day my mother came to pick me up from band practice. When she couldn't find me, she asked where I was, and the band teacher told her she could find me at football practice. When she got there to pick me up at the practice field, I was shocked to see her because I didn't think she knew I was there. I thought I could beat her home before it was time for her to pick me up from band practice. Now she knew I was playing football. My mother fussed at me on the drive home, but I convinced her that I was a better football player than a trumpet player. From then on, I played football.

As I progressed in my football skills, the coaches in town started showing an interest in me. My talent and speed would start to develop while I was still in junior high school. As a little boy, I had no clue about a gift in playing football, but I started understanding it a little in middle school. My junior high school coach, Jerry Pullen, didn't allow the younger players to play in the games. They had to wait their turn. I grew impatient watching the older guys play, so one day I asked the coach to put me in as a running back. He said no. I got mad and quit the team, because I knew I was better than any other player on the team, including the starting running back. After I quit, I realized what I had done and regretted my hasty decision. After a few days had gone by, I knew I had made a mistake and didn't like not being on the football team. I felt empty and naked without running with my football. Humbled, I decided to go back to football practice and ask the coach to give me a second chance. Coach Pullen did, and I was relieved. However, there was a catch. To get back on the team, I had to do extra sit-ups, pushups, run extra sprints, and do some exercises called up-downs. The punishment lasted a week, but it felt like a month because I was tired and my body was sore from all the extra work. I learned my lesson. I just had to wait my turn. When I was finally given the opportunity to play running back, I worked hard and did my best and excelled at running the ball. After I got my chance to play, I performed at such a high level that the high school coaches were eager for me to come up to the varsity team. I could hardly wait to get to play at that level, at Emma Sansom High School, the home of the Rebels.

Chapter 2
The Gift

My first year in high school, I was excited, because at the beginning of every school year, my mother bought us new clothes and new shoes. When I walked into the building as a freshman with my new clothes and new shoes, I knew the next four years were going to be filled with great expectations. Deep down I knew that I was on my way to pursuing my football dream as a running back on the 5-A level. I didn't focus on my size and what others were telling me about my small frame. I was doing all the right things while trying to make them see that size didn't matter if my heart was in it. I tried not to let their words distract me. It did hurt and get me upset when they made comments on my size, but I used their words to motivate me and push me forward in a positive way. My middle school football coach, Coach Pullen prepared us for the next level in high school. By pushing us harder than it seemed our bodies would allow us to go, out working the other teams, pushing us even harder when we accomplished a great play in practice and out-performing the guy we were up against in practice, he had us ready for the next level. Coach Pullen would keep us after practice to do extra repetitions and work on blocking and catching drills. It was hard work playing for Coach Pullen, but he knew what it would take for us to get better and succeed next season. He was a good man and looked out for us even when we were not practicing. He would pick up his players on the back of his pickup truck because we didn't have cars. If he didn't pick us up, most of us had to walk to practice or get someone else to get us there. Coach Pullen did what he could to get us to the practice field and then he taught us what he could. He had a "great nose" for evaluating his players and helping develop our talents. As a result of all the training, I was several grades ahead of my teammates and the varsity football players. I owe a lot to Coach Pullen for preparing me.

A friend of mine named Greg would pick me up almost every day of high school. He lived a block from my house on the next street. He was always hard on me and showed me tough love because he believed in my football talent, even with me being a little guy, standing just 5' 8" tall, and weighing 130 lbs. He said, using his usual profanity, "You better stay focused and continue to out-work the next guy on the field. Do your lessons and stay away from people who are doing the wrong things in life. You can be the best running back ever to come out of Gadsden! Do you $#@% hear me, Gene Jelks?" I would just listen to him and say, "Okay!" He was like a big brother to me; besides that, he was bigger than me.

The first day of high school varsity football practice, Buster Gross, the head football coach, and his staff divided all the seniors, juniors, sophomores and freshmen into groups by positions. I knew the returning starters would be selected to first team offense and defense. I was the new freshman coming in, and I had to earn a starting running back spot. The coach didn't call my name for a position. I was disappointed and upset. I walked over to the head coach and said, "I am a running back, and if you give me a chance, I can, and will, take your senior running back's position." The coach just ignored me and continued with his football practice. Again, I asked him to let me practice somewhere. To get rid of me, he told the defensive coordinator, Coach Nichols, to work me in as a nickleback in the secondary. I was confused because I felt sure all the coaches had heard about me being a running back when I was in the eighth grade. I thought there might be a possibility that the coach didn't know I was coming from General Forrest Middle School. Didn't he know that I was the one everyone called fast? I felt as if he thought I was too young, or too little to play football at the high school level. I finally did get my chance when the starting running back got hurt. My eyes lit up, and my spirit was jumping for joy. Of course, I was not happy about the player getting hurt, just thrilled that I was getting a chance to play. It was definitely bittersweet.

Since that day, my freshman year of high school, I always made the varsity team. But everyone wouldn't see me as a varsity football player because of my size. One day in my Biology class, the coach called for the varsity football team to report to the gym to get ready for a pep rally before a game. I got up out of my desk and started walking to the door to leave the classroom and my Biology teacher stopped me at the door. I said, "I am on the varsity football team." She said, "No, you're not." I said, "Yes, I am. I am the new starting running back." She told me to sit down. I got frustrated and told her in a bold voice to please go get Coach Buster Gross to verify I was on the team. She did. I shook my head and started laughing at her when the coach came back with her to the classroom to get me out of her class. Yes, I was somewhat disrespectful, but in my defense at that time, no one ever took me seriously when I said I was a football player because I was the smallest guy on the team besides the field goal kicker. It made me upset when she didn't believe that I was on the varsity team.

I would be haunted by another challenge because of my small size. People would bully me and beat me up. I still didn't like to fight even if the kid was smaller than me and I knew I probably could kick his butt. It was not in my nature to fight anybody. I was a laid back and quiet person who just wanted to go to class, get my high school diploma and then one day play college and pro football. Now, I wasn't a saint. I did fight a boy named Tim Keith because he talked about my mother in eighth grade. No one talks about my mother. She's a good mother. I got angry and hit him in his left jaw with my fist.

He fell like a tree. All my classmates told him, "You got knocked out by Gene." We had to go to the principal's office after the fight. The principal listened to both sides of the story. Fortunately, I didn't get suspended for my behavior. I would finish my freshman year with over a thousand yards and one touchdown. Why that many yards and only one touchdown? When we would get close to the red zone, the coach would put the bigger running backs in the game to score the touchdowns. That happens a lot in football.

I realized I had a gift and it was confirmed to me during my sophomore year in high school, partly because coaches, opposing players, friends, football scouts and other people around the state started saying, "This guy is super-fast and can do it on the football field." Because of my talent, I had grown as a sophomore and was now the starting running back. My belief in God and going to church was where my faith was while still continuing to work on my childhood dream. I would tell my friends, my family and other people about my dream and they would laugh at me and say, "You are too little to play football. Why are you dreaming so big that one day you will play for The University of Alabama and Coach "Bear" Bryant?" Even some of the coaches said I was too small to play football. Their comments did hurt, but I never let them see me cry. I would go off by myself to my back porch and sit on the steps and think about what people said. In the end, their comments only made me more determined. Even though at that time black athletes hadn't been playing at Alabama for very long, I never let that stop me from dreaming. I didn't respond to people's remarks. I kept focused and continued training and working on my running game. I heard in church from the preacher that Jesus died for me, and God loves all the children of the world: Red, yellow, black and white; they are precious in His sight. These words were all I had to hold onto besides my family's love for me, and so with that, I still continued to pursue my dream. At the end of my freshman year, I had rushed for over a thousand yards. An upperclassman cheerleader asked me to escort her to the prom. That was unheard of during that time. And I thought, wow! I was finally getting recognized.

My sophomore year I rushed for more than 1,000 yards and scored 12 touchdowns. My name was in the sports newspaper every Saturday morning, and sometimes in the headlines of the sports page. My recognition on the gridiron began to get other high school coaches' attention and the attention of college recruiters. One day my dad came home and told me that a coach at another high school wanted me to come and play for him, and he would buy us a house. I looked at my dad and said, "Are you serious?" I said, "Dad, you got to tell Mom about this." He told her about it, and she said, "He ain't going. He is going to stay right where he is." That was the end of that conversation. Momma didn't play.

My skills on the field were being sharpened and I continued to develop the natural talent I had been given. I would continue to improve, and my stats reflected the improvement. In my junior year, I received calls and college letters of interests from every top Division 1 school: Alabama, Auburn, Georgia, Tennessee, Georgia Tech, Mississippi State, Vanderbilt, and the list just kept going. After a while, I became overwhelmed with the phone calls. I was happy that my dream was coming into reality, but it was becoming stressful. I recalled the words of many people when they said I was too little and too short. They ignored me and laughed at me. Now, I was the talk of the town and Gadsden began to get noticed in a positive way too. I didn't talk to my parents about the letters I was receiving much of the time. I still had my senior year to go so I had plenty of time. I just kept reaching for my dream. Of course, through all of this, I still had to go to church, which was helping me spiritually. People who were not football fans would come to Murphy Stadium to watch me run with the football. Something clicked when I started getting major attention. The entire town started telling me that I was a great running back and a "hell of a football player." My home economics teacher, Mrs. Murray, told me I was pretty good and that I was doing well on the football team. She graduated from the University of Alabama. She was a very pretty lady. She kept up with all my stats from my freshman year up until that point. In fact, she was the one who showed me the list she had kept of all my accomplishments. I was blown away. It was a great feeling to be moving toward my dreams. To keep focused and not be concerned about everything that was happening, I told myself that all I had to do was to continue to improve my game and put myself in a position to help my family and myself. My goal was to prepare for the next season as a senior, and select a college to attend on a student athletic scholarship, so I could further my education and pursue my dream.

My junior year, I outperformed the upperclassmen. Every year the head coach would give out an award, a trophy for The Most Outstanding Athlete of the Year. That particular year, the coach had a tough decision to make. I received unanimous votes over a senior linebacker. As an underclassman, technically, I was not eligible to win the trophy; however, I had almost broken the state of Alabama's rushing record as a junior. The linebacker was good on defense, and I was good on offense. The coach couldn't share the hardware, so he stopped giving the award to the best player of the year. People in Gadsden started saying, "A lot of football teams at Emma Sansom tried to win a state championship long before Gene Jelks came along, and they were not successful." Around that time, some people were comparing me to Bo Jackson, which was a great honor to me.

In my junior year of playing varsity football, I finished the season with over 3,000 yards and 28 touchdowns, while still maintaining a 3.0 GPA. I started getting colleges' attention and recognition for my performance. My hard work was beginning to pay off. Before the games, I used to tell some of the girls that I was going to run and get a touchdown just for them. They loved it! That was my way of trying to flirt with them. I trained year round, running in the town where I was born. I believe that God gave me the "gift" of speed to make up for my small stature. I ran to stay in shape, ate the right foods, drank plenty of water and, of course, Gatorade! My high school coach told me he wished I could have played as an eighth grader. This was a huge compliment coming from Coach Gross. It had a special effect on me because it was then that I truly knew my ability was extraordinary. He said I had it all. I had tremendous physical talents and I was also a good student. That year, I played with some great players like Freddy Weygand and Andre Haley, just to name a few. The 1983 team was great. We ended up finishing a record 13-1. We lost to Escambia County in the playoffs. The score was 0-14.

We lost in the playoffs, but I will never forget the big game that had people talking for years. It was the opportunity the rest of the team and I had been waiting for; it took three years to come to pass. The biggest game in town was against Gadsden High School. They had a good football team, and the school was considered by most of the people in the town to be the best school to attend. It was where the middle and upper-class kids went who didn't go to private school. On a Friday night, we played Gadsden High, and I started at the running back position that night. Murphy Stadium was packed out. There was standing room only on the track. The crowd was so loud they could be heard for miles. Police security was beefed up because people would bet big money on both teams, and usually fights would break out, depending on which team lost. Back then we wore tear-away jerseys. I was wearing mine when I had my first big game against a considerably good defense with Aaron Pearson at linebacker. He went on to play for Mississippi State and in the NFL with the Kansas City Chiefs. I outran the defense. I had run all the way down to the 30-yard line from the line of scrimmage to be greeted by the safeties, and I lowered my head and split both of them and ran in for a touchdown. I jumped up and down in the end zone to celebrate my first touchdown on the big stage. That was a time and place I'll always remember.

Gene Jelks

After my junior football season, I began to run track. I ran the 100-yard dash in 10.6 but came in second to a guy called John-John from Gadsden High. He ran a 10.5. It was big news in the town. I ran track to work on my speed for football. In my freshman year, I played basketball at #2 guard to work on my footwork and quickness. I averaged 10 points and 3 steals per game. I was mostly known for my defense. I stopped playing basketball to concentrate on football. College football recruiters and other people started hanging around the practice field and after the high school football games, wanting to talk to me. For a small town country boy that was big to me, because there were no celebrities in my town to look up to at all.

My senior year I rushed for 1,500 yards and scored 15 touchdowns. We won the 5-A state championship, ending the season with a perfect record of 15-0. I had excellent teammates that year, and we had a great head coach, Buster Gross, along with some super assistant coaches. Coach Mike Shipp was my running back coach. He taught me techniques and pushed me beyond my limit. I valued my gift of "speed" because I was receiving college football letters from almost every college in the country. I received phone calls from football celebrities like Joe "Broadway" Namath and Ozzie Newsome from Alabama. That was unbelievably huge for me. The recruiters came to Gadsden and went around my community and asked people if they knew me. I remember the "411" and that if anyone told them, "Yes, I know him," they would give them gifts to give to me; I never took them.

One of my motivations for playing football was to receive a scholarship to attend college. My parents couldn't afford to send me to college, so I strived harder to get a scholastic or athletic scholarship. I would hear about other students taking the ACT and trying to score high enough to go to college. The only college that we had in our town was Gadsden State Community College. There is nothing wrong with going to a community college. I just wanted to go to a four-year college. One afternoon I told my mother that I wanted to be the first person to go to college in our family. She said, "Baby, I don't have the money to send you to college." I looked at my mother and froze. I knew I had to find a way to go to college, preferably away from home. I was motivated to work as hard as I could and win a scholarship in football, because without money to pay for college, I couldn't go. I knew I needed an education and a degree for the future also, and I had always been interested in Communications and Broadcasting. It was a good feeling to know that I was heading in that direction when I started receiving the letters from schools offering me scholarships. I was headed in the direction of my dreams.

Outside of football, I did have a social life, especially during the off-season. My girlfriend's name was Daphne Coleman. She was a junior when I was a sophomore. She was a "church girl" and a cheerleader on the Emma Sansom's cheerleading squad. Daphne was a sweet girl and would do anything she could for me. She invited me to the prom as a sophomore. As an underclassman, you couldn't go to the prom unless you were invited by a junior or senior. We spent a lot of time together at her parent's or my parent's house because there was not much to do around town as far as entertainment went. Tragically, she died in a car wreck. I was heartbroken. I will always remember her as the sweet, smart and pretty young lady that she was.

Regarding activities other than football, I didn't get out as much as some of my other friends, especially during the football season. After every game, my mother would pick me up at the team field house. She would only allow me to go to McDonald's and get some burgers and then I had to go back home. I couldn't go to a lot of parties or go out with the boys who were going out to talk to girls. My mother was a strict disciplinarian when it came to her children. There was only one person who she trusted to let me hang out with from time to time, that was my first cousin, Gene Lett. Some days I couldn't wait until he came to pick me up so I could get out of the house.

Gene Jelks

Growing up, I only had a few people I was close friends with because I was always playing football. As I got older, I was allowed more time to hang out with my friends. At that time my best friend Tang, which was his nickname, and I did almost everything together, including playing football. I would be over at his house a lot of the time. We would walk downtown Gadsden to buy him some school clothes at JC Penney's and then walk back home. Another good friend of mine, Steve Smith, would pick me up to go places with him because I didn't have a car. We hung out at a place called The Carver Community Center to talk to girls and listen to music. It was the hangout spot for the black teenagers. People would be drinking alcohol and smoking weed. We didn't smoke or drink. We just hung out to talk to girls. We were so broke we would have to scrape up change to put gas in the car. The police would patrol the area to make sure everything was okay. After spending time with our friends, Steve would drop me off at home, and he would head back to East Gadsden. That part of town was called the "Eastside."

As a football player, I did have many white friends, especially the fellas from the team. One night after a high school football game, I invited all the white players to our neighborhood to celebrate with the black players. It was the beginning of unity for us. They came to 10th street. We called it Tuscaloosa Avenue. We were talking about the game, socializing, and just hanging out. There were some of the guys, both black and white, drinking beer. I didn't drink so it was nothing to me what they did. The white players were dipping Skoal, and we were listening to all kinds of different music. The police drove by and broke it up because they thought the black boys were fighting the white boys. What a disappointment that was. We were just kids who were celebrating our victory together.

My senior year we had to play our rival team Gadsden High twice to make it to the next round in the playoffs. They were a good team too. Emotions were high on both sidelines. The game would go back and forth in scoring. It was one of the best and most exciting football games on the high school level that I had ever seen. We won the game; the score was 27-25. Next we would face Gardendale in Birmingham. Their offense and defense were both good on that cold rainy night. I think our defense stopped them on the last drive and our offense got the ball back late in the 4th quarter. We were behind, trailing 6-0. Tim Merryweather was our fullback. He carried the ball up the middle for about 7 yards, and then I ran the ball off tackle for a minimum gain, then a sweep right to me for about 8 yards. Their defense was tough and stingy giving up yards. We had one time to score with 14 seconds left on the time clock of regulation play. Coach Gross asked for a time out. In the huddle, he called a straight dive play to the right of the center and right guard. It was 4th and 7 in the red zone. The ball was on the 7-yard line. It would be our last chance to score. Andy Watts, the quarterback, handed the ball to me, and the fullback led the way up the middle. I ran straight up the middle behind my offensive line. I saw a hole so I ran low and hard as I could and I scored the winning touchdown! I give all the credit to the line and the fullback because I was not sure about running a run play with 14 seconds to go in the game with one chance to score. After the game, everyone on our team and our supporting fans started celebrating the victory. My teammates and I started cheering and chanting: "Gardendale tried, but Gardendale died." What a sweet victory to end my senior year in high school.

I finished my senior year with 1,700 yards and 15 touchdowns. My take on that year was, "Unity, teamwork and determination does pay off if you don't quit. Believe in your teammates and keep pushing toward the goal of becoming a champion on and off the field." My senior year was outstanding! Some highlights were: Graduate of Emma Sansom High School, Class of 1985; 5-A State Championship with a season record of 15-0; held the State of Alabama rushing record; won every high school football player of the week and gained national attention in Gadsden; selected to Dixie Dozen Top 10 Athletes in the state of Alabama; and, won many city, state and national football awards.

Overall, my high school journey was interesting. One girl who always had my back was Sabrina Green, a wonderful person; and, as one of my best friends, I always had her back too. I took college prep classes and became close friends with Brad Williams. We called him the "White Shadow." We played basketball together, and I would hang out with him and his parents. They would take me to the Coosa River to go riding in their boat. In the ninth grade, I had learned how to water-ski. That was new and remarkable because a lot of blacks didn't go to the river at all, much less, swim and ski. I enjoyed homecoming. It gave me school pride to see all the different classes that were building floats and then to see which one would get voted first place by the Homecoming Parade Committee. I was voted Best Athlete of the Year, along with a girl named Kelly Gross. I liked English; it was my favorite subject. We had a great principal, a great supportive administrative staff, and caring teachers who would take extra time with you if you didn't understand a lesson. Biology was interesting because I had never dissected an animal before. There were a lot of students who got high before classes started in the mornings. I had no desire to get high. There was some peer pressure from friends, but I was always scared of getting caught and being suspended from school. Besides, my mother would have beaten my butt and grounded me for wrong behavior in school, church or any place.

My four years in high school were pretty good. I maintained good conduct and good grades for the most part. I rarely received favors from my teachers because they believed in students earning the grades. I did get a lot of attention because of my athletic gift and it felt good getting compliments at school. My junior year I was voted Class President and Most Popular. I enjoyed the diversity of people at our school because we got a chance to learn about each other's race and backgrounds. My senior year I was worried about passing my

Social Studies exam. I had a "D" in the class and needed a "B" to pass and graduate. Thank God I did it. My journey with my classmates was a hell of a ride to graduation. We were a close class of over 250 students.

One thing that stood during my high school journey was that from my freshman year to my senior year, my status had changed from no one knowing my name to everybody knowing my name. And, it was all because of football. I was just Gene to my family and friends, but to others, I was "Gene Jelks the Football Player" who was destined to do great things in college football and possibly pro football. My family, friends and classmates said to me all the time, "You are a great running back." People on the street would recognize me and compliment me, even the white people, and that was new to me. I would even receive recognition from my pastor and church members. The spotlight was on me. I had Alabama Alumni taking me to lunch, and picking me up so I wouldn't have to walk anywhere because I didn't have a car. It soon dawned on me that I had what it took to play at Division 1 colleges.

Emma Sansom High School helped prepare me for the next chapter in my life which was to continue my education as a student athlete. The next phase of the dream was coming to pass. I was going to get to play for the University Alabama.

Chapter 3
Roll Tide

Once Alabama started recruiting me, everything in my life changed. I went from being a regular student to a local celebrity overnight. My high school teachers didn't say much to me until the college scouts started calling the school for me. After that, they started talking and socializing with me about things other than my class work or home assignments. One of my teachers was an Alabama Alumni. We would talk about other players on our team, and about life in general. She would bring me delicious desserts from home all the time. Another teacher would joke and laugh with me when I would sit in her office and talk about anything other than football, because the college recruiters were really starting to overwhelm me. One of my teachers would often give me a ride home from school, and if I needed something she would get it for me. I sometimes wondered if I had not been getting a lot of attention from colleges, particularly Alabama, would they have given me the time of day.

Even when I went on school visits to Alabama, I was given special treatment. The females would come out of the woodwork to try to talk to me. They were interested in me because I was a star football player being recruited by Alabama. I saw so many beautiful women who came out of the woodwork to get a glimpse of me. I met a girl through Bobby Humphrey at the dollar movie. In the beginning, we didn't hit it off, but we did exchange numbers. In the end, we started dating. Her name was Vertis. Vertis was a beautiful and intelligent woman. She was not a huge football fan; however, she supported me because she was my girlfriend. In my junior year, we got engaged. Our families got along well. She attended all my games with my family and after a home game both of our families would get together and socialize. We broke the engagement off when I went to Denver. I was heartbroken, but life goes on.

While I was being recruited by Alabama, I would get visits at my high school practice field from Rocky Felker, Alabama's running back coach. I had visits from my former middle school coach, now Alabama's assistant coach, Jerry Pullen, and an Alabama graduate assistant named Jerry. Jerry would call me on school nights and drive to Gadsden to meet with me in private at Noccalula Falls. He would ask me if I made a decision on which college I would sign with on college signing day. I told him I was still thinking and after that we ate Kentucky Fried Chicken and then just talked about normal, everyday stuff. The visits went on up until the Christmas holiday. Alabama State and Jacksonville State offered me scholarships. Eventually, the smaller schools said they could not compete with the Division One colleges, so they backed off from recruiting me. From then on, it was just Division One big schools calling or coming to see me. Jack Crowe, from Auburn, visited me. Auburn's head coach, Pat Dye, visited me after the championship game at my locker. We had just won the high school championship game against Gardendale and everyone on the team was celebrating. We talked for a few minutes about a scholarship and me playing for Auburn. Respectfully, I listened to him, but I finally said to him, "Alright, but I still have not made up my mind for sure yet, Coach. Can I just celebrate the 5-A state championship win tonight? Let's talk soon."

The recruiting process was difficult in some ways because I had a chance to sign with every college in the country. But my dream was to play for Alabama and Coach "Bear "Bryant. It would take me three official visits to Alabama, Auburn and another school that I can't remember. I would get visits from many coaches from small and big colleges. We would talk about what I wanted to major in, what kind of offense they ran, and which players I would have to compete against. I remember asking Coach Perkins if I signed with Alabama, would he give me a chance to start as a true freshman. He looked at me and said, "Yes, but you would have to work very hard and compete against guys like Kerry Goode." He went on to say, "I am telling you up front, I am recruiting Murray Hill and Bobby Humphrey too." I said, "Alright!" In my mind, I was up for the challenge. Coach Perkins was sincere and genuine when he recruited me. I liked that about him. To me, he is a man of integrity, class and honor. I thank God, Coach Perkins gave me an opportunity to earn a starting running back position and play for the "Crimson Tide."

My first visit to Alabama was on a private jet. I had never flown in an airplane. It was scary and exciting at the same time. In my mind, I kept thinking while I was on that plane, I am finally going to be in the company of the big boys and have a chance to play in Division One college football. I was going to be on national television and play in front of thousands of die-hard Alabama fans. I liked Alabama, or Bama, as the locals call the school because it had a home base style to it like I was used to in Gadsden. The football coaches were courteous and protective and made sure I wouldn't get into trouble on my visit to Tuscaloosa. The players were cool too, and very sociable. One of the players took me to a party, and I had never seen so many beautiful women in my life. There are many beautiful women in the South, and many of them go to Alabama. They also took me to another Bama landmark, Dreamland Bar-b-Que. It's located in a small country wooded area, and boy let me tell you, the bar-b-que there was so good it would almost make you want to slap your mama in the back of the neck! They were the best ribs I had ever eaten in my life! I did get a chance to visit Auburn. I met the renowned, soon to be Heisman Trophy winner, Bo Jackson. He showed me around on campus. He had my high school number 34 on his jersey. I wore my lucky number jersey throughout high school; however, he was the star football player at Auburn, so I knew I didn't have a chance to wear number 34 at Auburn. He was a super nice guy too. Although the recruiting process was stressful, at the same time it made me feel proud and special.

After being recruited by so many great schools, my dream of playing college football at Alabama was finally coming true. I had made my decision. I chose Alabama, which in reality, my decision had been made many years ago, but it didn't hurt to hear my other options. On signing day, a news reporter, Jimmy Smothers, my parents and I were sitting on the couch in the living room at my parent's house waiting for Coach Perkins to get there so I could announce publicly where I was going to sign. I was going to announce to the sports world that I was going to go to college and play for the University of Alabama. I was excited, and yet, very relaxed because the pressure that had been on me was about to come to an end. Another important reason I chose Alabama was that some day after my football playing days were over, I wanted to become a broadcaster and study communication. Alabama's communications department was ranked third in the country at that time.

On signing day, my dream to play for Alabama was fulfilled. Unfortunately, my dream of playing for the "Bear" would not come true. He died in 1983. I signed in 1985 under Coach Perkins. Coach Perkins took over as Alabama's head coach when the "Bear" retired. Still, I was thrilled because I was going to college on a full scholarship. My parents didn't have to cough up the money. All my hard work as a little country boy from Gadsden paid off. No matter how many people told me to stop dreaming big, I had to just keep going and telling myself "You can make it." I had to keep telling myself that until I reached my goal. My running ability and my natural talent for speed gave me the opportunity to go to college, but discipline, dedication and commitment got me and kept me there. It was hard work and believing in myself that brought me all the local, state and national high school awards. I had to remind myself of my abilities and awards when I went to Auburn and Alabama's football summer camps. They helped me evaluate my talent against some of the best prospects in the South.

My parents were happy that I was going to college on a full scholarship and that I was going to live out my dream; yet, on signing day, neither of them showed much emotion. I think they were too overwhelmed, just as I was, and the microphone and the news reporter didn't help. We were all a little nervous, as Jimmy Smothers was waiting to broadcast my announcement to the sports world. My father was a proud man because the values he taught me were paying off. I was told by people in the community that my father was telling people in Gadsden, all around town, "My son is going to Alabama." My high school coach, Coach Buster Gross, went to Auburn. I believe he wanted me to go to Auburn, but he never said anything to me, or tried to sway me either way. He just said, "Son, I am proud of you, and I really mean it. Wherever you decide to go, I am behind you 100%." My pastor, Reverend John M. Woods, was also happy about my decision. One Sunday in church, he announced to the congregation that I was headed to play college football for Alabama. I received a standing ovation from the congregation. He said, "Alright, he's now going to Alabama!" Everyone was saying, "We are all praying for you to have a good football career." Although signing for Alabama was a huge accomplishment in my young life, having my church family there and saying they were praying for me, kept everything in perspective. It was bittersweet for some, because the die-hard Auburn fans had mixed feelings about which team they would pull for now that I was going to Alabama. In the end, they were proud of me either way, if I chose Bama, or if I chose Auburn. My church family was full of good-hearted people who loved Jesus.

Gene Jelks

My family was happy and proud of me. My parents gave me a going away celebration party. My entire family was there. All I could do was thank God for the opportunity and for blessing my life. I was thanking God for everything. My dad was a proud man that day. My friends were happy for me too. They received scholarships too. Steve Smith went off to college at Jacksonville State, and Walter Smith went to college at North Alabama. I was glad for them. Both are exceptional men, and both went on to become pastors in the Gadsden community. Steve is now Pastor Steve Smith. He, and his wife, Lady Rita are pastors of New Destiny Church in Gadsden. Walter and his wife, Cynthia, are also ministers.

My last summer in Gadsden, I got a job at Marvin's Hardware Store working the yard, picking up customers' orders, and helping the delivery driver deliver items to customers. This was my first real job. While playing football, I never had the opportunity to work. Football kept me busy. It felt good working. A man should work. In fact, the Bible says that if a man doesn't work, he shouldn't eat. It felt great earning money to help my parents buy my new clothes for college. I continued to go to church and hang out occasionally with my family and friends. I didn't hang out much because I had to train and work out every other day before I reported to Alabama campus in the fall.

With all that was happening that summer, and even with all my accomplishments, I still encountered racism. It was during these encounters that I realized some people would just see others by the color of their skin. One day in that summer of 1985, the summer I graduated from high school and signed to attend Alabama, I almost didn't make it. It was a beautiful sunny day. My family was the first black family in an all white neighborhood. I became good friends with a neighbor's son. One day he asked me to go to the Coosa River boat dock with him along with another one of his friends. As we got out of the car to walk to the dock, out of nowhere five white men approached us and started saying, *"We are going to kill the nigga!"*

Walking Across The Bridge

My two friends jumped in front of me and said to the men, "Oh no you're not going to hurt him. Do you know who this is? This is Gene Jelks. The number one running back in the state and he just signed to play for Bama. You are going to have to fight us to get to him." I was frightened and in total disbelief that this was happening to me, especially because of the color of my skin. My two friends had to fight all of them while yelling to me, "Hurry up Gene! Run and get in the car, fast!" I did. I was like Forrest Gump… Run, Forest, run! But now it was "Run, Gene, run!" That was one thing I did know how to do. I had plenty of practice, yet I knew angels were with us that day and had to have helped them because my two friends whipped the heck out of those men as if they had stolen something! I thank God for sparing my life. I didn't think I was going to live to see my dream manifested, my boyhood dream of playing for Bama. I didn't understand the situation until my neighbors explained it to me in detail. They told me, "They are Rednecks, and they hate blacks." They were raised that way. My two white friends fought for me. That's when I knew everyone didn't judge me by the color of my skin.

I was hopeful that due to more people refusing to judge a person by his skin color, life was getting better for all mankind in the Deep South. That day my positive thinking on the matter was proven wrong; we still had quite a way to go. However, the civil rights movement had changed things for people of color and we, as well as people of every color, were healing with peace toward each other in the 80's. I had another race-related incident on I-59 in Gadsden during my sophomore year at Alabama. My truck stopped on the side of the highway on a hot summer day. I asked a man if I could push my truck into his yard until I could get my dad to come and help me fix the truck. He told me that it was all right with him. I thanked him and within the next few days my dad and I went back to get my truck. He told me that I owed him for storage. I said, "Sir, I am in college at Alabama. I don't have any money to pay you." He then said, "Well, boy, since you don't have any money to pay me for storage, I am going to have to keep your red truck. It's mine now!" My heart almost stopped beating. It wasn't worth the fight, but I never forgot that incident.

My last summer before leaving Gadsden for Alabama, there were a lot of parties, mostly club parties and occasional house parties. I wasn't allowed to go to any of them. My mother kept a close watch on her children, especially me. She knew where we were supposed to be at all times. We would mostly be with our grandmother, Mudear, or around our aunts and uncles' homes. I do remember going to one of my high school dances at the gym. I danced with girls and had to be home before midnight. I love my parents for raising us the right way. It kept us all out of trouble.

When I was packed and ready to go to Alabama, I remember hoping I wouldn't get homesick leaving my family as so many young people have done when they were away from home for the first time. I had to be at Alabama for reporting day on campus in Tuscaloosa. My parents drove me to Tuscaloosa. I had to report to the Bryant Hall dorm. Kermit Kendrick and I were the only two freshmen on campus at first. We talked and decided to be roommates our first year. He was a good dude, so it worked out fine with us being roommates. The next day, all the freshmen players had to report to the football practice facility to get fitted for our equipment. After that, we were introduced to our head coach and position coaches and given a big, thick playbook of Coach Perkins' offense that he ran. It was the pro set. The following day all of the freshmen would start the first day of fall practice. We would practice until the upper-class players reported back to campus. When the upper-class players reported to practice, I didn't get many reps like the day before. I would start off on the practice squad. Initially, I was disappointed, but I continued to work hard and to learn the new offense plays.

On the first day of training, the equipment manager, Mr. Willie Meadows, threw my jersey at me. He was one of Coach Bryant's guys. "Here is your jersey, Rookie!" he said. He scared me to death because he had this mean looking face. I got fitted for my equipment and then went into a team meeting with Coach Perkins and his staff. After the meeting, we went into a position meeting with our position coach, Coach Felker. He handed out playbooks and told us to "guard this playbook with your life." After going over the practice session, it was off to the practice field. We started out by stretching and then we did position drills, one-on-one and then seven-on-seven, and after that team drills. It was a hard practice because I wasn't used to practicing for two and a half hours. When the whistle blew, we hustled to get to the next drill. The heat was so intense on the Astro Turf's surface that it felt as if we were walking on the fires of hell. Every drill we did was on a speed of another level from high school. I had to get used to the fast pace of college football. The coaches were taking notes of who could play the first year to help Bama win another national championship. When the upperclassmen reported to training camp, all the rookies would be sidelined, including me, even coming in as the number one running back in the state of Alabama. It dawned on me that this wasn't high school; this was the next level. This was college football.

Alabama's tradition is so rich in producing champions; I wanted to be a part of contributing to help carry on the tradition. It was an honor for me to be in the company of such great champions and to be getting the opportunity to play for the Tide. The conditioning workouts with the strength coach, Al Miller, or, as everyone called him, "Killer Miller" was challenging; he truly earned that moniker because of his intense workouts for the Bama football players. I mean his training was hard. After training with him, all we wanted to do after being in the weight room was take a shower, eat, go to study hall with our tutor, and go straight to bed! In my opinion, and it still stands today, Alabama has one of the best football programs in the country.
Right away, I could tell a big difference. College football players were bigger, stronger, faster and quicker than the high school players. Here, everyone was number one at his game or position. I started

out on the scout team until Coach Perkins gave me an opportunity to compete for the running back starting position along with seventeen other running backs that year. We had some of Coach Bryant's players that carried over to the new Perkins' era. I mean we were loaded with tons of running backs: Kerry Goode, Chester Bragg, Craig Turner, Bobbie Nathan, Bobby Humphrey, Murray Hill, Bo Wright, and David Casteel, to name a few.

One thing I appreciated about the coaches was that they were tough, yet, respectful, and caring to all the players. Coach Rocky Felker stood out the most because he would always check on me and the other freshmen at Bryant Hall dorm after practice and at dinner. He would ask me my take on the game plan each week, and made sure I was well cared for being away from home for the very first time. All the coaches treated us like young men at all times unless we were not performing at the highest level, the level befitting an Alabama player. When we weren't performing at the top of our game, they could seriously chew us out to make us better so that we could become champions. Even when they did this, we were still able to maintain our dignity. But don't be mislead; Coach Perkins was strictly business in trying to win another national championship in 1985.

I felt grateful, honored, and excited about being an Alabama football player because they only recruit the best players in the country, the cream of the crop. It was a dream come true, and I continually thanked God for helping me make my dream finally come to pass, and in the end, size didn't matter.

Chapter 4
Sweet Home Alabama

College football is now America's second most popular sport, behind professional football. However, in much of the South, pro football can't compete with college football. Any given Saturday in the fall months, the streets and the malls are pretty much empty. Everyone is either at a game or watching the game with friends in front of a TV. In the last ten years, the South has been ESPN's top market for college football. It's been said that more people in Alabama watched Alabama play football than they watched the Super Bowl championship between two professional football teams. With that being said, Alabama doesn't need a pro team; it has college football. In fact, it has one of the most dominating football teams in college football history. If you were born and raised in Alabama, you know there are two teams to choose from: Alabama or Auburn. When people come to live here from other states, they are immediately indoctrinated and asked to pick a team.

Football in the South is right up there with good Christian values, going to church, fried chicken and, of course, sweet tea and Grandma's apple pie. For me, there was never a choice. I was Alabama true and true! Every fall, as a child, up until I played for Alabama, I was in front of my television watching Alabama play football and screaming "Roll Tide" at the top of my lungs every time they scored a touchdown. As crazy as it sounds, regardless of the tension between the races, or even the impoverished condition of the city, just watching Alabama football, for that three-hour span, made people a little friendlier. If Alabama won, and they usually did, walking to church the next day, or driving around town in the car, or walking the streets, it was obvious that the people's chests were a little bigger, and their smiles a little broader, as they greeted each other with "Roll Tide!" It's not as ridiculous as some may think; it's a pride thing…a Southern pride thing that no one will understand except Alabamians.

All I ever wanted to do was play football for Alabama. Regardless of who attempted to recruit me, my heart was, and still is, on the Alabama playing field. I believed the recruiters knew this, and it was their job to try to persuade me, but it was to no avail. There is nothing like being a football player for Alabama. That's why many players coming out of high school want to play for Alabama. The screaming fans that swamped to every game, the tailgating parties before the game, and as always the famous chant, "Roll Tide." For the people who have never been to an Alabama game, they are missing the treat of a lifetime.

Alabama plays its home games at Bryant–Denny Stadium, located on the main campus in Tuscaloosa, Alabama. It has a capacity of 101,821, and every home game, the capacity is filled with screaming fans dressed in crimson and white attire. It's the 10th largest non-racing stadium in the world and the seventh largest stadium in the United States. It's part of the Western Division of the Southeastern Conference, (SEC), which many will agree is one of the most dominating and forceful conferences in the NCAA. Alabama's football is among the most legendary and decorated football programs in NCAA history.

"As of the completion of the 2015 season, Alabama has 864 official victories in NCAA Division I (an additional 21 victories were vacated and 8 victories and 1 tie were forfeited), has won 29 conference championships (4 Southern Conference and 25 SEC championships) and has made an NCAA-record 62 postseason bowl appearances. Other NCAA records include 23 10-game or more winning streaks and 19 seasons with a 10–0 start. The program has had 34 10-win seasons (plus one vacated),[8][9] and has 35[b] bowl victories, both NCAA records. Alabama has completed 10 undefeated seasons, 9 of which were perfect seasons. The Crimson Tide leads the SEC West Division with eleven division titles and ten appearances in the SEC Championship Game. Alabama holds a winning record against every current and former SEC school. The Associated Press (AP) ranks Alabama 4th in all-time final AP Poll appearances, with 51 through the 2013 season."[1]

From 1958 to 1982, the team was led by Hall of Fame and legendary Coach, Paul "Bear" Bryant. Everyone loved the "Bear". After all these years, people still associate Alabama with the "Bear" and his famous black and white houndstooth or gingham hat and his deep voice. His many loyal fans continue to pay tribute and honor to him by wearing his famous black and white houndstooth on various clothing attire. "Bryant was not only loved by the people in and around the state of Alabama and the southeastern U.S., but by coaches all over the nation. John McKay, the legendary USC coach, had these words to say about Bryant. "He was not just a coach; he was the coach." Another quote about Bryant, from Bob Devaney, former Nebraska Cornhuskers head coach, is "He was simply the best there ever was."[2]

"Paul William "Bear" Bryant came to the Crimson Tide program in December 1957, after leaving his head coaching position at Texas A&M.[52] On December 8, five days after leaving A&M, Bryant was asked why he left for Alabama. Bryant replied, "Mama called,

---

1
2

Gene Jelks

and when Mama calls, then you just have to come running."[3] Bryant entered an Alabama program which had not had a winning record in four seasons. However, in his first season, Bryant led Alabama to a 5–4–1 record—one more win than Alabama had in the previous three seasons. In his fourth season, Bryant led the Crimson to their sixth national championship, which included Bryant's first bowl victory with Alabama.[4] Between 1961 to 1966, Alabama went 60–5–1, which included three national championships (1961, 1964, 1965), four Southeastern Conference Championships, two undefeated seasons, and six bowl berths."3 He retired at the end of the football season in 1982. Four weeks after coaching his last game, he died of a heart attack on January 26, 1983.

I didn't get a chance to play for the "Bear" but the moment I walked on the field that fall of 1985, I could still feel his presence. His legacy was the reason I wanted to play for Alabama. Practicing with such an elite group of players only made me want to excel even more. As a freshman, like any freshman football player, at first, you have to be tried and tested to see if you have what it takes to play at this level. To be honest, in the beginning, it was the most intense training I'd ever encountered since I started playing football. It was hard and demanding, both physically and mentally. Some people couldn't handle it, but I persevered and never let them see me cry, even when I wanted to cry. All the players were good, and I mean top quality good. After all, men don't get the opportunity to play for Alabama unless they are at the top of their game. But like I said before, everyone at Alabama was at the top of his game. So even though the next guy and I were friends, if we both had the same position, friends or not, only one was going to play, while the other sat on the bench on the sidelines. It wasn't personal, it was business, and everyone understood.

My first year at Alabama, I couldn't go up to the coach and say put me in because I am the best running back out there. They didn't op-

3

erate like that at Division One level. Like I stated, the coaches were gentlemen who treated all their players with respect; but we had to earn our way to play for Alabama. Just because we were recruited and attended the college, that was just the initial step; the next question was, "Can you play football?" One day Coach Perkins called me up with the first team offense. He called the same play in the huddle at least ten times. He was gut checking me to see if I was ready to step right in and play as a true freshman. Mike Shula handed me the ball every play and I got tired in a hurry. On a sweep right, the tackle missed blocking Cornelius Bennett and he hit me right at the line of scrimmage. I felt as though an 18-wheeler hit me and almost killed me. From that day on, I would step up my game to being on the level of the SEC. My hard work, endurance and patience eventually paid off. On game day, playing against The University of Georgia in 1985, Coach Perkins announced to the team in the locker room that I would be the starting running back. It was the happiest moment in the world for this 17-year-old boy. My first carry in the SEC was for seven yards. Mike Shula brought our team back from a deficit by connecting with Al Bell for the winning touchdown. The score was 20-16. Through hard work, determination, and much prayer and occasional talks with my parents when I could, I was finally going to get the chance to play in the "big one". I was going to play in the Iron Bowl in my freshman year, 1985.

The Iron Bowl is the biggest game of the year in the state of Alabama. It's one of the biggest, if not the biggest, rivalry in all college football. It's a game between two of the biggest college football schools in the SEC and the nation, Alabama and Auburn. During the week of the big game, all you hear is either "Roll Tide" or "War Eagle." For the fans of either school, it doesn't matter how well your team played that year, or how many losses or wins, if your team loses the Iron Bowl, it's a big deal for the remainder of the year. The winning team has the bragging rights until the next Iron Bowl. It's that serious! On an average, there are over 78,000 fans in attendance at the stadium,

Gene Jelks

and over 100,000 fans outside tailgating who are watching the game on portable televisions, or electronic devices. All you can see is wall to wall people; people are everywhere dressed in crimson and white or blue and orange. The media is everywhere too, on the field, in the locker room, at the announcers' table and the broadcast table. It's a sweet, beautiful mayhem.

I was nervous the night before the game since it would be my first Iron Bowl as the starting running back. It didn't help that I was going to play against Auburn's Heisman Trophy candidate, Bo Jackson. I met him earlier under friendlier terms, but now our teams were playing against each other. On my way to breakfast on Saturday morning, the day of the game, a little boy walked over to me and said, "Today is Bo Jackson's birthday." I said, "Really? Well, I am going to have to ruin his birthday today." I liked and respected Bo. We all did; however, it wasn't personal, it was football. I broke for a long run for 74 yards and a touchdown. Later, Bo went over the top for a touchdown. We came back on a drive that put ourselves in position for Van Tiffin to kick the winning field goal, which is now commonly referred to as "The Kick". I finished with 192 yards rushing on 18 carries. Bo Jackson finished with 134 yards rushing. It was a day I still remember as if it were yesterday. It was sheer pandemonium, or rather fandemonium, as thousands and thousands of fans got swept up in the joy of Alabama defeating Auburn. Bo Jackson went on to win the much-deserved Heisman Trophy, yet for that brief moment, getting that win was a sweet victory for my teammates and me.

The Iron Bowl was the game that brought me fame. At this point, as a big name athlete, I had to be careful with whom I associated. Girls were coming at me right and left. As I said, Alabama has a lot of beautiful girls, and an athlete can be greatly tempted. Being a big name on campus, students started to recognize and compliment me all the time. It did affect me, and I must admit I liked the recognition. What seventeen-year-old wouldn't? However, I was there to get an education. I enjoyed the fame, but I still had to go to class and study hall in the evening after football practice. I had a tough schedule and like all the other athletes, I had to learn to balance everything in college, particularly my social life. People would ask me for my autograph. That was new to me. I must admit, my pride kicked in, especially when I out-rushed the Heisman Trophy candidate, Bo Jackson, who went on to win the trophy that year. It didn't fully dawn on me what I had accomplished that day until I realized that I was the only player in college football history to out-rush Bo Jackson. That's when it hit me: I am famous. We went on to win the Aloha Bowl against USC. The score was 24-3. My freshman year, our record was 9-2-1.

The rest of my statistics for my first two years as a freshman and sophomore years as an offense running back were:

Rushing:

YEAR	G	ATT	NET	AVG	AVG	GAIN	LOST	TD	LP
1985	8	93	588	73.5	6.3	633	45	5	74 (AU)
1986	9	84	509	56.5	6.1	570	11	4	75 (VU)

Scoring:

YEAR	G	TD	PTS	Game Average
1985	8	5	30	38
1986	9	4	24	2.7

Receiving:

YEAR	G	NO	YDS	AVG.	AVG.	TD	LP
1985	8	12	195	24.4	16.3	0	51 (MST)
1986	8	1	4	0.5	4.0	0	4 (PS)

Passing:

YEAR	G	ATTN	COMP.	PCT.	YDS.	INT.
1985	9	1	1	1.000	2	0

Chapter 5
From Offense to Defense

Two major things happened during my sophomore year at Alabama; one would "rock" my world, the other one would "rock" my dream. It was a hot day in August, and we were all on the field playing scrimmage games. Out of nowhere, sophomore defense tackle, Willie Ryles, collapsed on the field during a blocking drill, hours later, he died. He was only nineteen years old. That was a hard thing to come to grips with because we were all like one big happy, but tough, family. And as with any family, when you lose a loved one, you have to find the strength from God to continue with business. Somehow we did. The other incident would have an effect on the way my life turned out for a long, long time.

Everyone knows in the sports world that Alabama football is the crème de la crème of football. It's never a surprise to the faculty or the players that some other team is always trying to recruit our coaching staff. Whether it's an NFL team or another college team, our coaches are always being approached. We had heard rumors that a team was trying to recruit our head coach, and that he was going to leave. Nothing was ever said to us, so it completely shocked us to learn that in the winter of 1987, Coach Perkins was leaving to coach an NFL team, The Tampa Bay Buccaneers. Talk about being floored! We, along with the entire school were in disbelief. Not only was Coach Perkins a great coach, but he was a great man, on and off the field. He treated us like sons; he certainly treated me like his son. I admired

Gene Jelks

and looked up to him with the utmost respect.

Coach Perkins came to Alabama after coaching the New York Giants in 1983. He replaced Coach Bryant, who had resigned in 1982. He had large shoes to fill, and even though Coach Bryant died unexpectedly within a month after retiring, everyone was still used to him and his charismatic coaching style. This didn't threaten Perkins; after all, he too was a player under the "Bear", and they had won two championships back to back. He was his own man, and in my opinion, he was right for the job. He had learned a lot under Coach Bryant. Immediately upon taking the position, he did two things. He changed Coach Bryant's wishbone offense to a pro-style offense, and he took down Coach "Bear" Bryant's tower. He coached Alabama for four years from 1983 to 1986, compiling a record of 32–15–1 and winning three bowl games. He holds the honor of being the only Alabama head coach to lead Alabama to a win over the Fighting Irish of Notre Dame for nearly thirty years.

In 1986, he had just finished a great year, 10-3 winning season, and recruited some of the best athletes in the country, so it was a surprise to many that he left. To this day, I still don't know why he left. Maybe he just wanted to go back to coaching pro teams. I don't know; I only know that his departure would change my life at Alabama. Coach Perkins would leave after the 1986 Aloha Bowl in Hawaii against the USC Trojans. It was bittersweet. We were happy for his new journey and wished him well, but disheartened by the fact that he was leaving Alabama, and us. That year I was the MVP on offense and Cornelius Bennett was the MVP on defense. I finished my sophomore year on a good note, and couldn't wait until my junior year. Little did I know at the time, my junior year would be nothing like my previous years playing football for Alabama.

Bill Curry replaced Coach Perkins. Players were surprised; in fact, the entire school was surprised, including the faculty. Many fans and

Walking Across The Bridge

spectators thought it was a big mistake to hire Curry because he was a Georgia Tech graduate and an outsider. Alabama wanted a coach that would carry on Coach Bryant's legacy. The players and many other people assumed Coach Perkins' replacement was going to be Coach Bobby Bowden of Florida State. The school was stunned when Coach Perkins left, but I think everyone was even more stunned with his replacement.

Like any incoming regime, or new personnel, we didn't know what to expect of Curry when he came in; and no one could blame us. It felt as if our father had left us. When he came in, we were silent and just looked at him. The coaches that were left behind were not happy because they were out of a job and had to find a new coaching job and relocate their family. The coaching styles of Curry were different than that of Perkins. To me, Curry's coaching techniques were different compared to Coach Perkins' pro-style techniques. However, whether the players liked the new coaching staff, wasn't the question. We were there to play football for Alabama, win all of our games and play for an SEC Championship, and then ultimately win another national championship. Therefore, we stayed focused on the overall mission. Yet, for my class, and the other classes that were recruited by Perkins, it was a much more difficult time because Coach Perkins personally recruited us, the Class of 85.

Things started changing at the beginning of my junior year. Positions were changing. I got hurt towards the end of my sophomore year. I was still starting, but Humphrey was getting the ball just as much, if not more than me. (This was brought on, as I would like to refer to it as "The Coaching Change".) As a result of this, my junior year would be significantly hampered by the coaching change. One sunny afternoon Coach Curry asked me to see him in his office. I knocked on the door, and he said, "Come in, Gene, and have a seat." He began to share some of his thoughts with me, and apparently they included changes. Changes that would affect me. I was not very happy with

Gene Jelks

how the conversation was going. He said, "You know I look at our defensive back department chart, and we don't have many cornerbacks." I just listened to him talk. The next thing I heard coming out of his mouth was, "I am going to put you in as a defensive back." I was devastated, and I just went numb. After being in complete silence for a moment, I finally said, "I was the starting running back for two years, and you are going to move me to defensive back?" Wow. "What a low blow," I told him. I said, "I could help out on defense until you bring in some more corners. I still will come back on offense and compete against Bobby to win my running back position back during spring practice." He ignored me and never gave me a chance to learn his offensive scheme. At that time, in my opinion, he forced me to play defense without looking at my past two years of film and achievements as a running back. I grew furious. I was forced out of my running back position and never given a chance to prove myself going into my junior year. Didn't he know that as a true freshman, I out-rushed Bo Jackson during the 1985 Iron Bowl? After that Iron Bowl of 1985, people said I had the potential to become a Heisman candidate. He never gave me a chance to prove to him that I had what it took to be the starting running back. It was terrible for me having to learn a new position that I had never played before in my life and my emotions were everywhere. I was miserable, especially since I was not given enough time to learn a new position at the SEC level, which to me is the toughest conference in the country. After he had finished telling me about my new position, I got up and left his office. Stunned and in total disbelief, I couldn't comprehend what just happened.

I only had so many practices in the spring to learn to play the position of defensive back. I told Coach Curry I was born to run. I needed to touch the ball. That was all I had ever done. He said, "What about the position of punt returner, kick-off returner or captain on special teams?" I agreed, and it gave me a sense of relief knowing that I would still be able to run with the football in my hand. I did

Walking Across The Bridge

everything I was supposed to do. I followed the rules. I made my workouts on time. I attended all team meetings, went to practice and excelled at whatever I was asked to do on the football field to the best of my ability. I asked myself, "Why me?" I didn't have an answer. My questions were, "Didn't the coach think I was good enough to be his starting running back? Did he think I was too small?" To be honest, after he changed my position, I wasn't happy at Alabama anymore. After my position had changed, Bobby Humphrey took over as Alabama's starting running back. To me, it wasn't right. It wasn't fair. My junior year was bittersweet at Bama.

The first time I played in my new position, I was playing right corner. My first career interception was against Southern Mississippi. I returned the ball 31 yards. That would set up David Smith hitting the receiver for 20 yards. Bama won 38-6. Against Tennessee, at Legion Field on special teams, I caught a punt and ran it back for 63 yards. At LSU, I picked off Tom Hodson. I believe I was number 6 in tackles, right up there close to Derrick Thomas' record. It was a long time ago, but I believe I was number 22 in interceptions. I led the nation in punt returns and was ranked number 2 in kickoff returns. My success in my new position only verified to me that I truly had a gift from God. I was a world-class athlete, and it was only God who gave my ability to me. In the Bible, Samson was the strongest man in the world, but as for me, I was one of the fastest men in college football at that time, and for whatever reason, Coach Curry didn't see this.

Things didn't go as well in my senior year. I was still playing on defense. I had some great moments, yet I had an injury that would again change the course of my destiny. We were playing against Temple. I returned a kickoff 96 yards to score a touchdown. At Vanderbilt, I had a 37-yard punt return and on the next defensive play, I was defending a tight end. When I forced him out of bounds, to avoid stepping on him, I jumped over his body. When I did that, all my weight shifted to the right side of my knee. I heard something pop in my knee. I had torn my right anterior cruciate ligament (ACL). My season was over for the year. Disappointment overwhelmed me. Later, in the fourth quarter, Bobby Humphrey would break his foot. His season would be over too.

With my injury, it was if I was starting all over again, but this time, it was not only physical, it was also mental. (I was healing in my leg, yet my mind wasn't healing from the change of position.) I had to take painkillers after the surgery. Maids had to come and clean my room every day and bring my meals three times a day. I got tired of people waiting on me so I called my mother and asked her if she would come and get me. I became depressed and felt empty because for the first time I could remember, I no longer had my goals to motivate me. My whole life had been one of running with a football, but I couldn't run on offense right now even if Coach Curry said I could. I believed that because of his decision to put me on defense, at a position that I had never played before in my life, I was now in excruciating pain, in more ways than one. I was accustomed to being banged up, or sore, but the severe pain I suffered after surgery was new to me. I could not take a shower; I had to just wash off. I couldn't sleep because of the relentless pain. I took the semester off, and during that period, I didn't work on rehabilitating my knee because the pain was unbearable if I attempted it. I finally returned to Alabama for my last year as a redshirt senior. We won the SEC Championship against the Miami Hurricanes. The score was 33-25.

I was still angry that Coach Curry had prevented me from playing my regular position, the only position I ever knew. The position I clearly remember signing up for when Coach Perkins recruited me. I was aware that the hurt was turning to bitterness, but mental and physical pain can do that to a person, and it was clouding my ability to think clearly. From that day on, Coach Curry and I didn't talk much, on or off the field. I stayed away from him as much as possible unless it was football related. I did go back to his office later and asked him again if he would move me back to my regular position on offense. His response this time was, "We are short on defensive backs. I am still keeping you on defense. At your small size, you will last longer in the NFL as a defensive back."

The start of my journey was coming to an end. Little did I know that the middle of the bridge would take me places where only God could bring me back.

At the Crossroad
(The Middle of the Bridge)

Chapter 6
When the Crowd Stopped Cheering

There comes a point in every person's life when he has to accept the inevitable. Unfortunately, mine was not so easy to accept because I still didn't understand what was happening in my life. I was still focused on pursuing the dream, my dream, the same dream that I had ever since I was a little boy. It was all I had ever thought about, that I would play football for The University of Alabama and then go on to play in the NFL. However, our life doesn't always turn out like we plan, especially when the Lord has His hand on us. We may pursue our dreams, but not fully understand that we may dream, but the Lord has called us each to His purpose. Our plans are not always the same as His plans for our lives. We have our dreams, yet, in the end, it's all about His purpose for our lives. It's at the middle of the bridge when we come to this realization. It's at the middle of the bridge when we decide if we are going to choose our will or His Will. During this period in my life, I was at a crossroad. I was at the middle of the bridge. I had a choice. Do I go back to the beginning of the bridge, or stay where I was and become stagnant? Or do I go forward in the other direction, toward the end of the bridge where I hadn't yet traveled? We often get to a place in our lives where we don't know how we got there. Looking back, we don't know how it all started. It could be an affair. It was harmless flirting that got out of hand, and now we are sneaking around with another person, telling lies to our spouse. It's a television show portraying slightly naked models, and now before we realize it, we are addicted to pornography. It was just a drink one night with the boys, and now we need a drink just to get through the day. Or, it was a dare from some friends to try marijuana, and now we're addicted to cocaine and heavier drugs. It just takes one time, one thought, or one incident to take you to a place, the middle of the bridge.

I will never forget that particular game. It was years ago, but it seems as if it were only yesterday. It was this incident that took me there, to my middle of the bridge. It was my junior year, and I was still upset about being switched to defensive back. It was that Vanderbilt game that I had the 37-yard punt return for a touchdown. Afterward, the defensive back coach asked me if I needed to rest before going back onto the field. I said, "Coach, I'm okay!" I was pumped, so he put me back in the game. On third down, I covered the tight end and forced him out of bounds. I landed in an awkward position on my right leg and tore my ACL (Anterior Cruciate Ligament). I tried to run back on the field to play defense, but I could barely move my right leg. I knew I had injured my leg, but I was optimistic that my injury was not career ending. That was until the trainers examined my knee and said, "You tore your knee up, and it will require surgery. You're done for the season." Hearing those words, I put my head down, devastated, I cried like a newborn baby. The trainer wrapped my knee in ice and propped my knee on the sideline bench for the rest of the game. As I said before, Bobby Humphrey broke his foot in the same game that day. Someone came up with a poster and titled it "Double Trouble for Alabama".

The MRI on my knee confirmed I had a torn ACL. My family was crying at the hospital. They were devastated that I had such a serious knee injury. They didn't care about me playing football; they just wanted me to get better. On the flight back to Tuscaloosa, the team doctor gave me pain pills to ease the excruciating pain from my torn knee. For the rest of the weekend, I popped pain pills like candy because I was in major pain and I would stay that way until I could make a visit to the team's orthopedic surgeon, Dr. Led Fowler, the following week. I stayed drugged up the entire weekend. The pain pills helped, especially when I tried to move my body around. This was the first time I had ever felt real pain. It was also the first time I began to depend on pain pills.

After I had talked with the head trainer about all the options I had for surgery, he said that the team's orthopedic surgeon, Dr. Led Fowler, would be doing my surgery. I didn't know anything about the doctor; the only thing in my mind was, is he the best? Naturally, I wanted the best orthopedic surgeon to operate on my knee so that I had the best chance to repair my ACL and begin rehabilitation to make a full comeback and start playing football again. I had heard about a Dr. Andrews, so I asked the Alabama head trainer if Dr. Andrews could do my surgery. He said that Alabama's team orthopedic surgeon was the one who did all the athletes' surgeries. (It turned out that Dr. Fowler did a great job on my knee. I was very thankful and blessed.) After the surgery, the coaching staff, players, family, friends and even some fans came to visit and brought cards, flowers and other gifts to show their support. I had a lot of support from the entire state of Alabama. They all showed lots of love and well wishes which helped me with my recovery from surgery. To this day, I'm grateful for their support.

I had a full body knee brace on my leg that I had to wear for eighteen weeks. The brace was set at a 45° angle. I couldn't do anything but wait until it was time to remove the staples in my knee from the surgery. When they took the staples out, I had to start the recovery process. The recovery process is painful and will make even the strongest and toughest person cry. The physical therapists want you to move your injured leg as if nothing is wrong with your leg. One thing people don't want to hear after this kind of surgery is to immediately start moving the injured leg. But this is necessary, and has to be done, if not, it will take longer for it to recover. Rehab is no joke! I had rehab morning, noon and evenings with the Alabama head trainer. I would do aquatic running exercises with a trainer so he could show me how to start getting the range of motion back in my knee. Learning to run again in the water took the pressure off my knee. The rehab was difficult and painful, like nothing I had experienced before. I had to put in hard work every day to build my body back up if I wanted to make a comeback.

I would get general treatment once a day. It was all part of the process. After weeks of getting checkups with the doctor, going to the training room for treatment, struggling out of bed and attending classes on crutches, I became tired and weary. I had a guest room at Bryant Hall on the first floor, because I couldn't walk up the stairs to the second floor to my assigned dorm room. I found myself having to depend on a ride from the personal cooks, the football players, the coaches, and friends. It became monotonous to fill out breakfast, lunch and dinner forms every day for eighteen weeks. The cook had to deliver my meals every day, the cleaning crew had to clean my room, and someone had to help me wash. I was bedfast for a long time. My life was stressful, and I felt alone. I was frustrated with it all. I had to wait weeks until the staples were taken out of my knee before I could take a shower. I didn't feel like eating. I began to lose weight, staying in bed resting and taking pain pills to tolerate the pain. These new challenges brought on depression, so I told the coach I wanted to go home to be with my family. I needed some downtime to think about my future football career. The coach agreed. I called my mother to come and get me. It was the best decision I ever made about the injury and my recovery. Alabama's training staff provided the best care for me to help me recover, but I knew if I were at home, away from all the distraction, my mind would get focused again.

When I went home to recover, I stopped my rehab for a semester. I just had to clear my mind. Someone was there to help me around the clock if I needed anything. There is nothing like your mother when you are not feeling well. When I went home, I felt safe. My family took very good care of me. It just felt right at the time. My relationships at home were good because my parents and family and I spent a lot of time talking, and we got along very well. My family made sure they cared for me the best they could. I would get visits all the time from my friends, family, pastor, deacons, and other church folks. My pastor, Pastor Woods, would come and encourage me and talk about Jesus to lift my spirits. The coaches did not check on me as much because of their schedules, but they did call.

I had a lot of emotions running through my head while recovering from my knee injury. My mind was full of questions: Will I ever play football again? Will I play recklessly again? Will I be able to make a comeback, to perform better, and be stronger on my knee? Will I recover my speed? Will I get over the mental shock of hurting my knee? Will I ever stop having flashbacks of the injury? Will I be able to compete and outperform my opponent? Will I hurt my knee again? Obviously, I still had a lot of mental rehabilitating to do as well. That was the second hardest part; it ranked right below the painful rehabilitation to my knee.

When I went back to Alabama for my senior season, I was not sure how my knee injury would heal. I dreaded going through rehab again because I knew I had to put in the hard work with the trainers, lifting weights and doing leg exercises to regain strength in my leg. After rehab, the trainer would ice my leg down or put my knee in a cold whirlpool to help keep the swelling down. I was disappointed because not only was I going to have to keep playing on defense, I was not going to be in the starting lineup on defense, and that's when reality set in. Coach Curry brought in a junior college defensive back name Efrin Thomas to replace me. I became a player's coach on the sideline, helping the defensive backs because of my experience. I felt anxious to get back on the field, but I was not ready to compete. It was a challenge to develop patience. I felt helpless standing on the sideline watching my teammates play in practice and in the football games. I tried to be helpful and hide the unhappiness I felt about not starting and playing in the games. Bitterness was knocking at the door, and before I knew it, I let it have access. The thing that stood out the most to me was the realization that from an early age, I took hits as a running back from pee-wee football all the way up to my sophomore season at Alabama and never had a season-ending injury. It was not my choice to move to defensive back, and in my heart, I felt that if I had to get an injury, I would rather have been injured while in my natural position as a running back. I never in my life experienced this kind of damage while playing football, and maybe if I had been allowed to stay in my position, instead of being forced to play in a position I wasn't accustomed to, maybe, just maybe, I wouldn't have been injured at all. And that's when, unknowingly, I let the enemy in the door.

I developed resentment toward Coach Curry and Bobby Humphrey. I know it sounds childish and prideful, but at the time, it hurt me to see him in the position I enjoyed for so long and also seeing him in the spotlight, knowing that we both should have been sharing time in the backfield because we both were great running backs. Bobby was the bigger back with power, and I was the smaller back with blazing speed. We balanced each other. To me, Coach Curry gave me a raw deal, and Bobby took advantage of his opportunity and broke a lot of records at Alabama. In my mind, I though that if I were given the opportunity, I, too, would have broken records and been one of Alabama's all-time great running backs. It is easy now to see how the enemy was having a field day with me. At the time, in my mind, I didn't see anything wrong with my thinking or my feelings.

The more I allowed these thoughts free reign in my mind, the angrier

Walking Across The Bridge

I became. I was furious that Coach Curry forced me to defensive back so Bobby Humphrey could rack up great stats and run for the Heisman. I did get jealous of that. To me, Bobby was getting some of my attention and had been given the chance to run for the Heisman. I became even more resentful towards Coach Curry. (He never explained to me why he moved me until nineteen years later.) With these thoughts continually running through my head, I became miserable at Alabama, and with Coach Curry. We didn't have a good relationship after he changed my position, but now it was nonexistent. I kept my distance as much as possible. The assistant coaches were good coaches. My position coach was a good defensive coach. He was a cool guy, a friendly man who had a lot of football knowledge. I still wasn't happy on the defensive side of the ball because I was out of position, but the defensive coach made it bearable.

My last year at Alabama was not as great as my previous years. I would be number two on the players' department chart. I was still recovering from the injury from my junior year. Recovery was a slow process after having major knee reconstruction for a torn ACL. The coaches slowly worked me in the game plan on special teams and my role was the nickel defensive back on third downs on defense. I returned punts only, and for the most part, I watched the games from the sideline. When the fans stopped cheering for me, I knew my college football days playing for Alabama were now just memories and in the history books. Things felt weird. It was a lonely feeling not hearing 75,000 Bama fans cheering, or screaming, out your name in the Bryant-Denny Stadium. It felt weird not getting to play and be on national television each week. That was when reality started kicking in, and I had to ask myself some questions. My main question: What were my options now? I concentrated more on going to my classes and to study hall. I took a heavy load of class hours because a football career in the NFL was uncertain for me now. I majored in Communications, with a concentration in Advertising and finished my minor in HCA: Speech. I had one semester left to complete, but I had a decision to make in the spring: Wait for the NFL draft or finish school. I decided on the NFL draft. I wanted to go pro.

Alabama won the SEC Championship during my senior year (1990) under Coach Curry. I received a championship ring. I was happy about the championship. It was an honor to be on that SEC Championship team. We beat the University of Miami in the Sugar Bowl in New Orleans in the Superdome. After the season was over, I just went to class and continued to work out until pro day tryouts at Alabama. All the NFL pro scouts came on the same day to check out the college football players. My agent, Jerry Albano, advised me not to go to the combine, which was held in Indianapolis that year. He thought I wouldn't have a good workout because I was still healing from my knee injury. I sat out of the combine and I worked out at the gym to stay in shape for my upcoming workout for all the NFL pro scouts. My workout during pro day on the Alabama campus went all right, but my 40-yard dash time had decreased because of my injury. My normal 40-yard dash time was 4.27. Pro day I ran a 4.5. The pro scouts had me on the player scout list at the defensive back position instead of a running back position. I was disappointed, and my mind got the best of me again. I really thought that Coach Curry messed me up real good, even with me trying out for the pros. I worked out for the NFL scouts as a defensive back. Now it was just a waiting game until the upcoming NFL draft. Coach Perkins came back to Alabama and met with me and told me I had a good chance of being picked up by a team but he didn't know which team. I thanked him for the information and the confidence he still had in me. I continued to train at Alabama with Alabama's head football athletic head trainer, Bill McDonald and personal trainer Coach Terry Jones. Coach Jones put me through a serious weight program Monday through Friday, and also a strenuous cardio program until the draft. He was my strength coach during my junior year and because of him, I led the nation in punt returns. He was a great guy and a super player's coach at Alabama.

Walking Across The Bridge

The first day of the 1990 NFL draft, I was at my parents' house watching it on television, waiting to hear my name called. I didn't receive a call from a team the first day. I was now beginning to worry that I wouldn't be going to the NFL. The next morning I got out of bed, ate breakfast and was still excited that I had another day to get a chance to go to the NFL. After what seemed like an eternity, my agent called and informed me that Denver selected me as a walk-on candidate. I wasn't officially drafted, but to be given a chance as a walk-on candidate for a team such as the Denver Broncos was still a great accomplishment. My emotions had me jumping for joy. My family and friends were also happy for me. I remember keeping a big smile on my face that day. My hard work from rehab paid off. (I say to anyone who had to face any adversity, challenge, or obstacle to never give up. No matter what obstacles you face in life, never stop dreaming.) I waited by the phone for the personnel of operations from the Denver Broncos to call me to make it official. Someone finally called and gave me all the information over the phone. I was informed of the date I would have to report to Denver for rookie camp and that I would have to pass the physical exam before I could sign my contract with the organization.

Up until the day I left for Denver, I continued to train and work out. I still wasn't up to my full potential with my knee, so I did everything I could to help strengthen it. If I wasn't training or working out, I kept busy. I was positive and hung around positive people. I continued going to church and serving God, just as my mother raised me to do. I got a call from Bobby Humphrey, my college-playing buddy. Denver drafted him in the first round of the supplementary draft the previous year, 1989. He asked me why I didn't call him to tell him I was coming to Denver. I told him I had a lot of things going on personally, particularly with my knee, and getting it prepped to go to Denver. We talked a little more about football and other stuff. I told him how proud I was of him and all that he had accomplished at Denver and that I would see him when I got there and we could hang out. But when I finally arrived in Denver, we didn't get a chance to hang out that much, because things were different for us now; things weren't like they were when we were playing ball together at Alabama. He was on the team; I was trying to get on the team. One night the veteran players took all the rookies out on the town. Bobby and I had a slight disagreement, but we were cool and professional about it. However, we never shared the brotherhood camaraderie that we shared at Alabama.

I left Alabama in the spring of 1990 going to Denver, Colorado to report to rookie camp. I arrived in Denver and met with the head coach, Dan Reeves, and the rest of his coaching staff. There were thirteen rookies including Shannon Sharpe. All rookies went to meet with Coach Reeves in the film meeting room. He gathered us all together and said, "Welcome to the NFL men. You are among the best football players in the world." I felt as if I were in a dream because I was sitting here in the same room among the best football players in the world. After the coach's motivational talk, all the rookies walked to the training room for a physical. There were doctors at different stations checking all our body parts with all kinds medical machinery of the highest caliber. They hooked us up to these machines, checking our bodies for any kind of flaw. I passed all my physical tests, so the next step was to meet with the finance department to discuss my contract. Coach Dan Reeves was a good conservative coach. He had a good kind heart, but he was direct and firm. The coaching staff was some of the best in the business. I was familiar with some of the coaches because they were with me when I played for Alabama and for General Forrest Middle School. Coach George Henshaw was my offensive coordinator at Alabama, and Coach Al Miller was on staff as the strength coach. In fact, he was on Coach Bear Bryant's staff as his strength coach before the Bear died. I also had my assistant running back coach, Coach Jerry Pullen, from Alabama, on Coach Reeves' coaching staff in Denver. I signed on to play as a defensive back and punt returner with the Denver Broncos. I wasn't given an option about the position. Since I came out of Alabama out of position as a defensive back, I felt as if I was pushed into the NFL out of position. I only had one year of experience at defensive back. My mind was still at that place, where I felt robbed, and for that reason, it blinded me to the fact that I did make it to the NFL as a running back. That was my dream. If only I had been able to see the clear picture and had not focused on my anger and the injustice done to me, and focused on the positive, what I had really accomplished, I would have realized an important fact: I played in the NFL in a position that I had only learned after my sophomore year in college, not my previous career, which is not a common feat. I wouldn't understand or appreciate this until years later.

Charlie Waters was the defensive back position coach. He played for the Dallas Cowboys. In camp we did defensive back drills, one on one drills, seven on seven drills and then team drills. We had to do a 40-yard dash test. We had to run 40 yards 10 times and make our average the same time we ran for the pro scouts during pro day 40 times and we had less than 90 seconds between each run. We were required to make a 90 percent average, or we would fail the test. In the weight room, it was mandatory that each player completed 90 percent of the workouts. If we were late for team meetings or curfew, the head coach would fine us. Everything in the NFL is based on money, business and winning the division, and ultimately winning the Super Bowl. I was not used to playing in a high altitude, not to mention snow and freezing cold weather. It was difficult to breathe because of the mile high altitude in Denver. We had to train in one foot of snow. I will never forget that because my chest was burning so bad from running with less oxygen than normal; plus we were training at a very fast pace on every drill and the team drills. We had two weight training sessions: one in the morning, and one in the afternoon. We could choose one or the other. I would work out in the early workout session with Coach Al Miller. We had good trainers for the injured players. The teammates were pretty cool, except one that I didn't get along with very well. I met John Elway. He didn't say much, but he was a heck of a quarterback. Man! Did he have a rocket for an arm! I remember that I broke a training camp record on the high box jump for doing a lot in one minute. It was a quick jump box drill to test our quickness.

Everything was going well with me until an incident with Coach Waters. Charlie Waters asked me a question one day in the film room about coverage on the practice field. I began to explain what the coverage was, and how I was beaten on a play by one of the wide receivers and I was giving my best effort to recover on the play. Well, it turned into an all-out argument and after that meeting in the film room, we never talked again. We didn't get along from that day forward. Coach Waters had a discussion with Coach Reeves and then Coach Reeves called me into his office one day and told me he was cutting me from the team. My heart stopped beating for a second. I walked out of his office, cleaned out my locker and left the football practice facility. Hurt, dejected and in total shock, I left with my spirits lower than a squashed bug. That's how low I was. All I could think about was what was I going to do? My dream of playing for the NFL had just died.

My life would be different after I was released from the Denver Broncos. I didn't have a backup plan. I was living off my earnings that I had made in the NFL while searching for my next career opportunity. I felt lost not playing football. I realized when reality set in that I was back in the real world. From being on top of the sports world as a star football player to the bottom as a fallen star, I was devastated. Ashamed and embarrassed to have to go back to Gadsden and have people look at me and ask me why I am not playing in the NFL any longer, made me sick to my heart. I just got sick of having to answer people's questions. I decided it was time to get a nine to five job, even though I knew I wasn't cut out for that. I went back to Alabama and started teaching at a middle school in Gadsden. Telling myself

I could make a difference in children's lives, yet, in my mind, I was thinking how to get another shot at the NFL. I became depressed and unhappy with my situation. Then, out of the blue, on a Saturday afternoon, I was surprised to get a call from the Canadian Football League asking me if I was available to come and work out for the team, the Winnipeg Blue Bombers. I said, "Yes, sir!" I hung up the phone and said to myself, "Yes! That's what I'm talking about!" I went to church the next morning to worship God, and the next day, Monday morning, I flew to Canada.

When I arrived at the airport in Canada, personnel from the Winnipeg Blue Bombers (CFL) organization met me and we drove to their football facility. I met the head coach and the defensive back position coach, signed my contract, and went to work out for the coaches on the practice field. I had to learn the playbook quickly because the season had already started. The next game against Calvary, I started as a defensive back, with 20 seconds left in the half. I was covering a wide receiver for Calvary, Doug Flutie dropped back to throw a pass to the wide receiver and he caught the football in the end zone for a touchdown. I was traded to Saskatchewan Roughriders where I finished my professional football career and retired. I knew then it was time for me to give up the dream. My body and speed were no longer at the level they used to be. I returned to the United States and began searching for work. I did odd jobs for a while and then started working for the school system in Alabama. I missed football. It was driving me crazy that I was no longer playing professional football. It took me about ten years to find peace about this.

When a player is used to fans cheering for him and then one day they stop, the silence is unbearable. Ask anyone, a professional sport's player, or even an actor or an actress, what happens when the cheering stops. Many will say they miss that applause, the adulation, the praise, and the "Atta Boys." The silence is not golden; it's deafening. If we are not careful and don't have a backup plan, we would do anything to hear those cheers again. And I mean anything. When the fans stopped cheering…that's when I allowed "IT" to take me there.

Chapter 7
First Comes Pride, Then the Fall

"Be sober, be vigilant; because your adversary the devil, as a roaring lion, walketh about, seeking whom he may devour:" 1 Peter 5:8, KJV

When you think someone owes you something, and you have a chip on your shoulder, trying to prove something to yourself and to others, that's when the enemy comes in and takes over your heart and mind. That's when you are liable to do anything because your emotions are running rampant and you can't think straight. You are not looking to God for the answer; you are looking at yourself for the answer. And like a mouse focusing on getting the cheese, he doesn't see the cat until it's too late, and now he's trapped. He has no way of escape. Thus, the end is inevitable.

The enemy may or may not be the cause of the situation; he doesn't have to be, he just waits for you to take the first step. He is waiting for you to go for the cheese. He takes advantage of your vulnerabilities, your low-self esteem, your feelings of being wronged, your anger, and your bitterness. He is watching, waiting and prowling around to take advantage of you because his mission is to kill, steal and destroy you (John 10:10). He is proficient at taking advantage of our feelings, because if we are honest with ourselves, we are not always controlled by the facts or the "Truth"; our feelings control us. It is easy for us to get our feelings hurt, ignore the facts, and proceed to deceive ourselves with our truth. After all, our truth is the truth. This is what happened to me.

I had just retired from the CFL. I came back to the US feeling as if I had just lost my best friend. My football career was over, and I didn't know what to do. All I ever wanted to do was play football as a running back. I knew it would eventually come to this, the end of my football career, but I never imagined it would end like it did. That was it. One day while I was still trying to figure out what to do next, a man came to my parents' house and asked to talk to me. He said he would return within a week. When he returned a week later, he said, "I have something to show you." I said, "What is it?" He pulled out some cancelled checks that had been written out to me by an Alabama booster. I felt as though I had seen a ghost and just stood there on the porch. Right then, I knew what I should do, but like Eve listened to the serpent, I continued to listen. He knew what bait to trap me with, my pride, my hurt, and my vulnerabilities. He played with my ego and my emotions. He said, "Alabama ruined your running back career and gave Bobby Humphrey your glory." Empty and alone, broken and defeated, I wasn't seeing or thinking clearly. All I could think about was what he did to me. I was blind-sighted. That's when my demons kicked in, and I got angry all over again for what Coach Curry did to me. The anger was dormant, but when he spoke those words to me, it resurfaced. I was not mad at the University of Alabama, alumni, or the Bama fans. I was angry with Coach Curry for forcing me to the defensive back position. In my anger, I couldn't see the trap; all I could see was the cheese. And like anyone who is filled with anger, bitterness or is hungry for retribution, I went for the cheese, and like the mouse, what happened next was pretty much like a death.

I told my parents about the man approaching me with the cancelled checks and my parents immediately said, "Whatever you are thinking about doing against Alabama, boy, don't do it!" The rest of my family told me to keep quiet, be cool, and move on with my life. However, the thought had been planted in my heart, along with the seeds of bitterness, and from there I was trapped with nowhere to go. My feelings were controlling me. A man from Gadsden picked me up and drove me to Atlanta to meet with an attorney in his office. There were several people there in his office that day. They were all waiting for me. They had the cheese for the mouse. They had phone numbers of the people I was supposed to talk to and a tape recorder there to record the conversations. A person was there coaching me on what to say to the people on the other end of the phone line. They called the people, not me. When they called the Alabama coaches for me to talk to, they recorded the conversations. It was all planned out, a set-up, and I played right into it. I know my anger got the best of me, and it caused me to lash out at anyone I thought had hurt my chances of playing football at Alabama and at the pro level. I regret my actions and that my bitterness got the best of me. Yes, I did take money; I did get paid. Back then, I didn't see what I was doing was wrong. In my twisted thinking, as a young, immature man, I believed what I did was right. Now, I know it was not the right thing to do. Today, I am not proud of what I did, but that's what happened.

When the allegations hit the media all over the country, ESPN, CNN and USA Today covered the story. People couldn't believe what I did, especially my close friends and family. My family didn't know anything about what happened until they heard it on the news. Eventually, I did tell my family and talked with them about what I did. They were disappointed and hurt about the choice I made, but it was too late. The damage was done, and unfortunately, in the aftermath, the damage included my family. I received death threats and so did my family. I was blackballed. No one would talk to me and as a result, I put myself and family through some difficult times. People stopped speaking and associating with them because of me. Some players did try to reach out to me, but their attempts were futile. David Gilmer, an Alabama offensive lineman, called me and we met in his car to talk about what I did, and how to make it right, but I was too angry and blocked out what he was saying. Hoss Johnson, another offensive lineman from Alabama, who also blocked for me during my time there, contacted my mother concerning me, but I had nothing to say to either one of the brotherhood guys. I had made up my mind that I would get revenge on Coach Curry.

The irony of the entire scandal was that the cancelled checks surfaced because of a divorce. One of the parties was an Alabama booster; the other was an Auburn alumni. While I was dealing with my own anger issues, I allowed someone with their anger issues to have an effect on me. In my defense, I did call the appropriate people to inform them about what happened. I didn't get a return call from them. In my impatience and irrational thinking, I assumed that the people at Alabama had turned their back on me, so I turned my back on them, which only made things worse.

Being wiser now, I know that I was being used by a small group of Auburn alumni to start an NCAA investigation at the University of Alabama because by now my eligibility at Alabama had ended. During the investigation, nothing was found, but it would open the door for an investigation on Antonio Langham, who talked to a sports agent after the 1993 Sugar Bowl. As a result of this, Alabama was put on probation, and the NCAA sanctioned the football program for three years. The team was also banned from postseason play the following season. Although my part didn't lead to the disciplinary actions against Alabama, it did trigger the investigation on Antonio Langham's infraction.

The whites, the blacks, alumni from Alabama and their associates cut all ties with my family and me. Alabama fans stopped asking for my autograph, and everything that had my name on it, autographs, posters, pictures, and programs were destroyed or taken off the walls.

Walking Across The Bridge

I was the most hated man in the state of Alabama. After getting the death threats, I was scared for my life. I was worried about my family's safety, so I felt it was best if I left the city. My name was all over the country on newspapers and television. My name was mud! There was nowhere for me to hide in the state. Atlanta was an up and coming city. People were doing their own thing and were not focused on me so I thought Atlanta would be a good place for me to live. I moved to North Georgia, close to my attorney, Stan Kriemer, who was handling my part in the investigation. I felt fearful, but continued to remind myself that God would protect me.

Someone hired a woman to follow me and try to get close to me as revenge. The woman called my attorney's office and told him she was pregnant and having my baby. It was a lie and a scam. The next thing I knew, her attorney contacted my attorney to discuss the matter. I told my attorney I didn't have any sexual relations with the woman. I didn't even know who she was or what she was talking about. I was mad because I smelled a rat. My stress level was through the roof and I stayed nervous. I became paranoid and jittery, all the while watching my surroundings. I never left my townhouse unless I went to my attorney's office or had to walk to the grocery store. Stan advised me to write the woman a check so the problem would go away because the Alabama scandal didn't need to draw any more attention to me. I couldn't handle the pressure, so I started drinking again to fill that void. Everyone slammed me for betraying Alabama. I wouldn't talk to the media because I was afraid for my life. I never gave the media a chance to talk to me in person or over the phone because someone might be able to trace my whereabouts. I played it safe.

I never was a drinker or used drugs. My first time using legal drugs was when I injured my knee. But now with my life threatened, alcohol became my solace, and eventually drugs too. My first real encounter with illegal drugs was when I was in Denver. I was around drugs, but never used illegal drugs until I went to Denver. One night

I decided to stop at a convenience store to buy a six-pack of beer. I drove up to an associate's house, contemplating on whether I was going to try a beer or not, so I took the beer in his house and offered him and his friends a beer. I noticed a funny smell in the air. As I greeted everyone they spoke quietly and they were all looking like zombies. I knew something was up, but I could not quite put my finger on it. Then I asked a question, "What's up with y'all looking so sad?" No one said a word. Then my associate asked me if I wanted to try some cocaine. I said, "Sure. I will have a little." We ran out to get some, but they didn't have any money. I pulled out a one hundred dollar bill to buy some. That was the night I started drinking and doing cocaine. I didn't use cocaine again until eight months later. It started out as a social thing. At first, I did not like the effect that cocaine had on me. After the sports scandal, drugs and alcohol become part of my everyday existence.

I finally went back to Gadsden when my mother told me that my father was diagnosed with lung cancer. (He was diagnosed a year before he took an early retirement.) I spent the rest of the time with my dad and my family until he died. The news had consumed me with sorrow. I prayed to God to let my father live. No one in my family had ever received this kind of bad news. My dad and I didn't talk much about his illness because he didn't want to worry his family. I do remember my father telling someone else that if you had never had cancer, don't wish it on anyone. My little brother saw my dad suffering great pain. My dad told him he was ready to die. I went to talk with my father, trying to encourage him that everything was going to be all right and to just hang in there. I felt helpless because I couldn't help my father or ease his pain.

I started back drinking heavily and using cocaine to fill the emptiness in my heart at the thought of my dad dying and to forget about the sports scandal. I made a mistake and then kept making more mistakes with my bad decisions. This went on for months. I realized it was an evil spirit, but I couldn't stop using drugs. I would go on binges for three days, drinking and using cocaine. When I got broke, I would walk to my parents' house, get some food to eat, take a shower, and rest for days. I continued this cycle. On my father's deathbed, he noticed something was wrong with me. He told my mother that he believed that I was on drugs. My mother asked me if I would come and sit down in the living room and I did. She didn't fuss at me, but she said she was concerned about my problem and that I needed to get help. I finally agreed to go to rehab at Bradford Health Services to treat my drug dependency problem.

Knowing my dad was dying, and the hurt and pain I caused my family over the investigation scandal, I completely lost it. I used cocaine to ease my problems, but the drugs made things worse. I became irritated easily and rude to my family. I would drink a 12 pack of beer every other day. On a positive note, I did help my mother take care of my dad after his chemotherapy treatment. The doctor told our family that my dad only had three months to live. I was heartbroken. There was nothing else the doctor could do, but we still hoped for a miracle. I planned a trip with my dad after his last chemo treatment. I drove him to his family's old home place where he grew up in Glencoe, Alabama. We stopped along the way and got an ice cream cone. We talked and laughed a lot. We talked about old times as I cried silently, knowing my dad was dying. Tears dripped on the ice cream as the knowledge sunk in that I was losing my best friend. I'll never forget the day he died. Early one summer morning, it was on a Monday, I was asleep in my parent's bedroom. The phone rang, I said, "Hello!" It was my mother. She was crying softly. "Your dad died early this morning in his sleep." I sat straight up in the bed and told her, "I am on my way to the hospital as soon as I put my clothes on." I drove to the hospital in a pool of tears. I went into the room and saw his still body, and started rubbing his head and sobbing. It was the worst day of my life. I regret my father didn't get the chance to see me get my life straight with God. I attended my father's funeral with my mother, sister and two brothers along with the two grandchildren. People all over Gadsden, black and white, sent flowers and cards filled with money. They brought food and other gifts to help my mother. For this, I was grateful and so very thankful.

Now that my dad had died, I made the decision that I was going to be on my way to get the help I needed. Even though he was no longer with me, I wanted to make good on a promise. I wanted to get well and delivered from substance abuse. Before I went to get help at a rehab, my favorite aunt who lived in California died. I started grieving and crying for her. I put off getting the help I needed and started using drugs again to numb the pain in my heart. The day of her funeral, I was dreading laying her to rest, though I knew she had gone to be with the Lord. She was my inspiration and always knew when something was wrong with me. I would deny something was wrong because I did not want to her to worry. She always knew. After the burial, the family went back to the church. The church staff fed our family and all the guests. After leaving the church our family went to our grandmother's house to comfort each other. My uncles and I were talking in the back yard, and after a while we all went in the house with the rest of the family and friends. Something quietly spoke to my spirit, "Go back outside in the back yard." I eased my way back through family in the living room, the dining room and the kitchen. I opened the back door and walked out on the back porch and began to reach down in the cooler for a soda, but a soft voice said, "Look out on the left side of the roof." I did. There was a huge owl sitting on the roof. I stared in disbelief! I ran back into the house and told my mother, "There is a huge owl on the back roof. Come look!" My mother said, "Boy, you are just lying!" I didn't give up and went to my great aunt sitting at the dining room table. "Annie there is an owl on the back roof. Please come see for yourself." She got up out of her chair and went to see it with me. As she looked up at the roof, Annie's eyes widened in surprise as she witnessed the owl for herself. She said, "Oh my God!" I said, "Annie, I told Mom, but she did not believe me." Annie went back into the house and made the announcement. "Y'all, Gene ain't lying! There is an owl on the back roof." Everyone went to see the owl, and started talking all at once. They said, "We have never seen owls in the area before."

Over the next several days, I was getting ready to go to rehab. My heart was grieved by the loss of my Aunt Paulene and the death of my dad. I went to rehab for thirty-one days. I had a black counselor. We met in his office. I was an emotional wreck, tore up, from the floor up from drinking and using cocaine. He said, "I watched you play football. You were an amazing world-class football player and I know who you are, or who you used to be. You are no longer a star football player; you have a problem." I started crying because I knew he was right. One summer night in rehab, the guys in my cottage were outside sitting around talking and drinking coffee before curfew. I don't drink coffee, but for some reason I decided to walk down to the cafeteria and get a cup of coffee. All the guys had gone inside. I noticed as I was walking back up to the cottage, it looked like the same huge owl on the front of the roof. It gave me "chills" when I saw it for the second time. I never shared it in rehab because I thought the staff would have admitted me into Brice Hospital, the mental institution in Tuscaloosa. Some say, seeing an owl is a bad omen, but to this day, I will never know why I saw the owl.

After rehab and the death of my father and my aunt, I had to go underground for six years because the Alabama sports scandal was still big news and it was too dangerous for me to remain in Alabama or anywhere in the Southeast. Since my life was in danger, I relocated to California.

Chapter 8
Under the Bridge

In 1996, I went back to rehab, but this time in California. I got my life back on track and got a job. I worked in California for five years and was enjoying my life; however, in 2001, I was tired of being that far away from home. California was nice, but it was nothing like the South. I decided to relocate to Atlanta to be closer to my mother and the rest of my family. Atlanta was a nice fit for me. It was close enough, but not so close that I still felt the heat of the scandal, or so I assumed. I was in for a rude awakening. I realized that football rivalries run deep in the South, but little did I know that so do football ties. In the South, football teams and fans cross the state lines and become cordial when there is a break in the tradition of the game, or if someone goes against the unspoken rule or norm. The teams play each other on the field for the win, but just like any family, an outsider can't come in and make waves; it's just not done in southern football. Rival teams will stand together against a rule breaker, especially a whistleblower. So, even though I thought Atlanta was a safe haven for me, I learned the hard way, that my previous actions still had severe consequences. My name was still blackballed. I couldn't get a job anywhere.

For three years I didn't socialize in Atlanta. I was literally afraid for my life. When it was time for me to renew the lease on my townhouse, I decided not to renew it. I called my attorney and told him I had nowhere to go. He met me at the Marta train station in Briarcliff, we talked briefly and he gave me $100. That was the day I became homeless. I didn't have anyone to call in Atlanta because no one would associate with me. I was terrified about my situation and lonely from being isolated. I took the train downtown looking for shelter. I didn't have a clue where to begin looking for a place to go. I walked to the park and saw people with bags and started blending in with them. They were homeless too. I asked a man, "Where do the homeless people go?" He gave me some names of some people and some streets. The first night being homeless would be one of the worst nights in my life. To add salt to the wound, I had missed the cutoff time to enter a shelter, so I had to sleep on the steps of a church near Underground Atlanta. The next day I was hungry, so I followed the homeless crowd from a distance to a nearby center that fed the homeless every day. I ate there for several months. I started panhandling for change on the Georgia State campus around lunch time. I did that for a year. In the evening I would walk to Grady Hospital and with a tin cup in my hand, I would panhandle the doctors and nurses for money.

I had no running water to take baths or showers. I felt as if the world had turned its back on me so I turned my back on the world. I reached "Rock Bottom". My world had come tumbling down. It crashed hard; I went from being on top of the world as a star football player to falling into a dark abyss. I fell deep. I fell hard. I was so alone. When I was at rock bottom and really started feeling alone, or thought I was alone, and felt that no one cared for me, it took me to a place, which in a natural, sane mind, cannot be comprehended. It's a place between normal and abnormal, a place between sanity and insanity, rational and irrational. It's a place where somebody can go either way. Unfortunately, for too many, when they reach this point, they go to the deep end, and sometimes, to a far off place of no return.

I felt so alone that I just didn't care anymore. I didn't care whether I lived or died. I felt as if my life was over. I became suicidal after sinking that low, and I looked for some relief. Alcohol and drugs were my escape; they were my relief. I ended up in a distant city, separated from my family and friends. To relieve my loneliness, and feed my habits, I began to wash car windows on the streets for money or for a bite to eat. One day a man and a woman pulled a gun on me and stuck the barrel of the weapon in my chest. I saw my life flash before my eyes. I thought they were going to shoot and kill me on the street. I was going to die in this state. Another time, a homeless man pulled a knife on me because he thought I was too close to his area. One thing I had to learn fast was that there are protocols everywhere and the homeless people were no exception. I went to the park on Auburn Avenue, where all the homeless people hung out. While there, I went to the bathroom on the street and the police saw me. I just started urinating on the street in the middle of the day. It got to the point that I just didn't care. I had no shame. A police officer came over to me and asked me why I was going to the bathroom on the street in the middle of the day. I told him I was homeless and had no place to go. He asked me what I thought he should do. I said, "Officer, I am guilty, so do your job." He then recognized me, but not as Gene Jelks, the football player. He said, "Oh, you're the homeless car wash man." I said, "Yes, sir." He said, "I am not going to take you to jail. I want you to wipe down my police car and we'll call it even." I ran over to his car and wiped it down. He then asked me to clean his personal car at the station. It was only God who kept me out of jail that day. From that day on, I began to wash his friends' cars too. With this newfound confidence and boldness, at the sports bar and grill on Auburn Avenue, I started asking the wealthy patrons if I could wash their cars while they went into the restaurant to eat. Some people would ignore me, but there were some who would let me wash their cars for a few dollars. Month after month, especially on the weekends, I washed cars and my reputation grew as being the homeless car wash man. In fact, I hired two other homeless people to help me on

Gene Jelks

Friday nights at the club. I was doing better and could almost smile as I recalled having another car wash business, along with my pecan business, back in Gadsden so long ago. My business grew, but one day the police came out and stopped me from washing cars because they were getting complaints from some of the customers. That was the end of my car wash business.

I would beg for food at the club. Other times, the patrons would pay me to park their cars. Some would tip me for watching their cars while they were inside, while others just looked at me with disgust or sympathy. There were some who wouldn't look at me at all; they were ashamed and felt sorry for me. At times I would hold up a sign with the word 'homeless' written on it. I would sit by the highway with my sign and a cup asking for food and money. My life was spiraling down even more. I was arrested for being homeless twice while trespassing through the parks. One winter night, it was raining and I had no place to sleep. I walked over five miles seeking a place to get out of the rain. I came up to a construction site where they were tearing down some projects. I climbed over the gate and looked for a place that appeared safe enough in one of the projects in a closet. I found some old newspapers and covered myself with it the best I could. The freezing rain leaked through the roof and dripped on me throughout the night. The next morning I awoke to some loud noises. It was a bulldozer tearing off what was left of the roof where I had been sleeping. I jumped up and ran out of the building as debris hit me on the head and shoulders. I could have been killed, but God was on my side and protected me.

Being homeless was so different from the way I had become accustomed to living. At home, I always had a warm bed to sleep in, a hot meal, and a cozy place to live. My family and friends, the people who loved me, always surrounded me. Trying to learn how to survive on the streets was hard. I never knew this kind of life existed. No bed, no water, no stove, no heat, no air conditioning, nothing but the clothes on my back. In the past, when I used to see the homeless, I would see them, but not really see them. Now I was one of them. This realization made me sorrowful. The homeless people minded their own business. They did their own thing. Homeless people didn't speak to each other much, and if someone was not in their clique or crowd, they looked at them as the enemy. Also, they could be cruel. Sometimes they would say bad words to me. It was definitely, every man for himself in this environment. Each day I lived to survive because the next day was not promised, not in life on the streets. I was pretty much a loner as a homeless man, except when I had drugs or alcohol. Then, everyone was a friend, that is, up until it was gone. When the drugs and spirits were gone, it was back to every man for himself.

When I would sleep in shelters, I was threatened and sometimes the other homeless people would steal what few items I had. They would always try to "punk" me. It was a constant battle. There were a lot of mean people in shelters, and there were a lot of fights, stabbings and rapes. A man got killed in a shelter where I stayed one night. There were a lot of sinful things going on all the time. Without living this way, it's hard to comprehend what being homeless is like. There is nothing, and I mean nothing beautiful about being homeless. I ate out of the trash cans. I went to soup lines. I went to the park on the weekends where churches would feed the homeless. I begged people on the streets for money and asked people at restaurants to buy me some food because I was homeless and hungry. I did everything you see the homeless do because I was homeless.

At night, I slept in abandoned buildings, behind businesses on the weekends, shelters, on church steps and under bridges, in the woods, on benches, anywhere I could find some rest, that's where I would sleep. And yet, even then, I didn't sleep through the night because I always had to watch my back. Living on the streets is a dangerous and stressful place to live. There is a silent code, and everyone knows the code like they know the protocol. On the streets, anything could happen, and I mean anything. The homeless, both men and women were always getting hit on by men who were looking for some action. It was a fact. Men approached me to sleep with me. This was nothing on the streets. This was a normal, typical day. This was disturbing because I had been molested at an early age, and at night was when I was tormented by that incident.

One hot sunny summer day I walked to the food court at the Underground Atlanta. I was hungry. I had no money and hadn't eaten in several days. In this state of mind, anyone could become desperate, and desperate means whatever it takes, do it. I was desperate and hungry; therefore, I didn't care. I walked around the tables looking for leftover food to eat and then I looked in the garbage cans for food. As I left a trashcan, a man walked up to me and said, "I know who you are. Come on and I will order you a hot meal and a drink." I accepted his offer. We sat down and began talking while I ate my meal. That man was a former NFL player for the San Francisco 49ers. I thanked him, and I thanked God with a sigh of relief for the meal. Some homeless people knew who I was and asked me what happened to me. I told them society had blackballed me, and without a job I was forced to be homeless.

I was sleeping at the Underground Atlanta under a bridge on a cold winter night; the temperature was five degrees outside. Boy was I cold! The police came and pointed their flashlight in my face. They said I was trespassing. I told the officers I didn't have anywhere to go so they could just arrest me. They made a deal with me. If I see or hear of some fugitives they were looking for I would let the police know, and they said there was a reward for their arrest. I agreed and thanked the officers for not running me off or arresting me. It was so cold I was shivering as I walked to a club trying to panhandle some money, but things were slow, so I walked back to the bridge, got under it and that's where I slept. I was very hungry. I got up and started walking down the railroad tracks only wearing a shirt and a pair of

Walking Across The Bridge

blue jeans. I walked over to a dumpster and started digging through the trash looking for food. There were big rats running all over the dumpster. I didn't find any food to eat and my body was so cold that I was going into hypothermia. I had hit worse than rock bottom. I walked back to the bridge where I had been sleeping, and got under four dirty blankets where I still felt as if I were freezing to death. Something just clicked in my mind. I got on my knees and started praying and crying out to God. "God, if you are real, would you save me? Would you help me get out of my mess? I am sick and tired of being sick and tired. I give my gifts and talents back to you so you can use them for your glory. I have sinned against you and shamed my family and hurt a lot of people. I will stop running like Jonah did and surrender and help children like you have called me to do, and please God send me one of your servants." After I had prayed this to the Lord, I went to sleep. I was cold, but for the first time in a long time, I felt a little peace. That winter night was when I decided that I didn't want to be homeless anymore; something inside me snapped. I came to my senses as I was looking for food in a cold dumpster. I had no heat to keep me warm and from freezing to death. I did not want my family to find me dead under a bridge. I didn't want people to remember me as a homeless man.

I went to an outreach center in downtown Atlanta the next day and asked for help. They told me a church was coming to feed the homeless at six that evening. I would have to come back then. I went back at six and went to the church service. It smelled like a dead dog in the building stuffed with homeless people. After the service they fed us a hot meal and the minister interviewed thirteen people, including me. That night would change my life. I was the only person the minister took into his outreach. The church outreach was called Nspire. Only God! It only took seven days for God to answer my prayer. I stayed in the outreach for one year and stepped out on faith. Nspire took me in the program for one year until I could love myself again and provide for myself. A minister named Greg provided me with new clothes, food, a job and an apartment, as well as transportation to work. I had a job cleaning buildings for three years. I walked to work summer, spring, fall and winter. I was able to save up enough money to get an apartment.

In 2007, two things happened to me that would change my life. I had a heart attack, and I was reunited with my daughter. I was just getting back on my feet from being homeless, working and just trying to get it together. I was not feeling well, and out of nowhere, I began to feel numb and began to experience chest pains. I was having a heart attack. Years of abusing my body with cocaine and alcohol had finally caught up with me. My enzymes were dangerously low from drinking every day and using cocaine. To make matters worse, I was malnourished due to the lack of a proper diet. I thought to myself, just when I'm finally getting it together, I was going to die. My fear of being remembered as homeless, an addict and a drunk was coming to pass. Those were my thoughts, but God was about to change my path and the heart attack was part of the process, and part of the plan was reconnecting with my daughter.

Any man will tell you that a son is a father's pride, but a daughter is a father's joy. Every daughter wants to be a "daddy's girl" and every father wants to be a "Knight in Shining Armor," a "Hero" in his daughter's eyes. My daughter and I had an estranged relationship. Her mother and I were young when we had her. Things didn't work out, but we remained cordial for the sake of our daughter. When everything turned crazy in my world, I just left. I ran. I escaped. In my departure, not only did I leave my family, I left my daughter without a father. One thing I could say about my parents, until the day my father died, both of them were always there for me. I could count on both of them, through the good and bad times. Even with what happened, they were there for me. They still loved me. My daughter could not make that statement; she couldn't say that I had always been there for her.

My daughter and her mother were living in Atlanta at the time I was homeless. I was ashamed, so I never contacted her. I was in the hospital for three days before the hospital contacted her. When my daughter came to the hospital, she was a nervous wreck. She was concerned about her dad. I didn't want her to see me in this condition. She sat with me and her eyes were sad and troubled. I thanked God that she was by my side. She bought me a prepaid cell phone to keep in contact with her. When the doctor released me, I had nowhere to go but to a shelter or back to the streets. My daughter had her own responsibilities. I was just glad she was supportive; that was enough. I didn't want to go back to being homeless, but I had nowhere else to go. I spent a night in a shelter and during the night someone stole my cell phone. I was mad and fed up with dealing with the many spirits around the shelters. I told my daughter what happened. She got upset at me and hung up the phone. We didn't talk for a while, but God moved in her heart. She let me move in with her. It was a big relief off my mind. I now had a place to call home. It was a time for me to reconnect with my daughter and my grandchildren. While she went to work, I babysat my grandchildren until she got off work. I did homework with them, made lunch, helped clean their rooms and the rest of the house. It was a great time for all of us. We played in the back yard. They rode their bikes, and we took long walks. Sometimes my daughter would let me drive them to the store. I began to go to church on a regular basis with them as a family. I was having the best time of my life. I didn't know it at the time, but God was positioning me from under the bridge to walking on the bridge. It took a heart attack to bring me out from under it. Only God!

I was homeless in 1995. I was homeless again from 2001-2008. About 400 homeless people were living on the streets of Atlanta when I was homeless. At first, I believed in my vain imagination that I was in this state because I couldn't cope with the death threats from the sports scandal, and because of this, I was blackballed. No one would hire me for a job. However, while living with my daughter, and going to church and reconnecting to God, I realized that I took myself there. I allowed myself to go there, "under the bridge," because I was bitter and angry. I allowed something that happened to me years ago to fester in my heart. I was still upset that Coach Curry forced me to change my position. The Lord wanted me to deal with it in 1995. I didn't. I ran. I escaped. Therefore, from 2001-2008, He allowed me to choose my path. My path led to living under the bridge.

I learned that through all of my challenges and struggles, I found out that God has made us for Himself. He created a place inside of us that only He can fill. You can try to fill it with alcohol, you can try to fill it with drugs, you can try to fill it with sports, you can try to fill it with fame, and you can even try to fill it with money, but it still does not lead to fulfillment. I found out that I was empty before Christ came back into my life. There was one other thing I knew I had to do. I had to make amends with myself and with others.

Chapter 9
The Prodigal Son Returns

There is a story in the Bible that talks about the Prodigal Son. It is found in the Gospel of Luke 15:11-23 (KJV). It reads:

And he said, A certain man had two sons: And the younger of them said to his father, Father, give me the portion of goods that falleth to me. And he divided unto them his living. And not many days after the younger son gathered all together, and took his journey into a far country, and there wasted his substance with riotous living. And when he had spent all, there arose a mighty famine in that land; and he began to be in want. And he went and joined himself to a citizen of that country; and he sent him into his fields to feed swine. And he would fain have filled his belly with the husks that the swine did eat: and no man gave unto him. And when he came to himself, he said, How many hired servants of my father's have bread enough and to spare, and I perish with hunger! I will arise and go to my father, and will say unto him, Father, I have sinned against heaven, and before thee, and am no more worthy to be called thy son: make me as one of thy hired servants. And he arose, and came to his father. But when he was yet a great way off, his father saw him, and had compassion, and ran, and fell on his neck, and kissed him. And the son said unto him, Father, I have sinned against heaven, and in thy sight, and am no more worthy to be called thy son. But the father said to his servants, Bring forth the best robe, and put it on him; and put a ring on his hand, and shoes on his feet: And bring hither the fatted calf, and kill it; and let us eat, and be merry: For this my son was dead, and is alive again; he was lost, and is found. And they began to be merry.

The funny thing about the story of the prodigal son, it's not just about the son, but it also tells a lot about the father. The father knew everything about his son. He knew his ways, his issues, his arrogance, his pride, and his ego. However, he also knew that deep down, he was a good son who needed to come to himself. He knew that it would take the son going to a place of total destruction, a place filled with misery, hunger, shame, and despair for him to see the truth.

In the story of the Prodigal Son, the son told the father, "Father, give me what is mine." Now, without realizing it, the son insulted his father by asking him to give him something that really didn't belong to him, but that the father should give it to him anyway. The insult wasn't just that he was asking for it; the insult was asking for it while the father was still alive. It's like our kids asking for their inheritance while we are still alive. Inheritance was given, especially in that culture and time, when the parent was deceased. To ask his father for his inheritance, while he was still alive showed that he had no concern or compassion for him. The truth is an inheritance is not ours until our parent is no longer living.

Although the father understood this, his love for his wayward son moved him with compassion to give the son what he asked for. The father gave the son his, not the son's, money, and allowed him to go away and spend it the way he wanted. Any good parent knows that if a child is immature and filled with pride, he will not spend money wisely. This is what happened with the prodigal son. The prodigal son did exactly what his father knew he would do. He spent his money on his friends, loose women, wine, or anything that he found pleasurable. Then the unthinkable happened; the son came to a place where he no longer had any money. With no money, went the friends, the women, and the wine; in my case, the drugs. Gone was the lifestyle that he was accustomed to living. He found himself in the pigsty, or in today's terms, homeless, hungry, begging, and eating the pig's food; in my case, eating out of garbage cans. He eventually got tired of this lifestyle, and tired of eating from the pigsty. One day, through prayer, he came to himself. He remembered his father, and his father's house, and that he had treated his father poorly, so he made a deal with himself, "I shall go home and be one of the servants because I am not fit to be called my father's son."

The father saw his son when he was a great way off, which suggests the father was continually looking for him. When the father saw the son in a far off distance, the father shouted for joy and ran out to greet him and hug him. He called for a ring for his finger, shoes for his feet, and the best robe for his son. He told his servants to start the preparations for a big celebration in his son's honor. He told them, "Get the fattest calf, the most expensive wine, and enough food for a king." They were preparing for a banquet because his son had come home. It's interesting that when his father came out to meet him, the father, rather than lecturing him, he embraced him, and started shouting, "My son was dead, but now he is alive!" The son left the father, but the father never left the son. The father believed that one day his son would come back. He knew that his son was made of good stuff; he came from a good family, so he just waited patiently until his son came to himself.

I was the son in this story, and the father was the Heavenly Father, God. I was a son who was so full of anger and pride. I allowed my ego to get the best of me. It took me to a place that I would've never imagined I would go. I was in the pigsty eating pig's food. I was angry with Coach Curry for changing my position. I was angry that I didn't get a chance to compete while playing in my usual position, the one that had gotten me the scholarship, and that I had forever missed the chance at a shot at winning the Heisman Trophy. I was angry that I got injured and ruined my last year at Alabama and the chance to become a legendary college football player. I was angry that I had allowed others to control my destiny. I was angry that my father had died of cancer. I was angry that I had been molested. But more significantly, I was angry with God. "God, why did you allow this? Why did you allow all these bad things to happen to me?" For the moment, I didn't see that many of these things that happened to me weren't because of other people, but because of my own actions stemming from my anger.

All I could remember were the glory days back in high school and my first years at Alabama. I was a star Alabama football player. I thought if I did all the right things people would reward me; however, my thoughts were wrong, especially since I had no control or power over the head coach who was making all the final decisions for all of us. I never expected this, or saw it coming. I was in denial, telling myself I had the right to be angry. I had the right to be upset. Look what they did to me, this poor, black country boy. I had been done wrong. I was so messed up in my thought process, that I believed all of this. I was so deceived that I actually believed these things were the truth. The anger within became a death to my spirit and soul.

My anger built up in me each day like water coming to a boil on a stove. My mind kept replaying that fateful day, and all the events after that day, when Coach Curry switched my positions. My fury just boiled over, and my temper blew like the teapot whistle blowing when the water has boiled. I lashed out because my dream had been cut short. I blamed Coach Curry, and anyone else who I felt had done me wrong. I developed a bad attitude toward people that I normally would be nice to, including my family and friends. For nineteen years I was bitter, and I viewed and judged people as if they were all Coach Curry. I couldn't get past that incident, and that caused my pain and suffering. In my mind, life should have been as I had envisioned it back when I was on track at Alabama, projected by some pro scouts to be a first round draft choice once I became eligible for the NFL. I dealt with my emotions of anger, bitterness and resentment toward Coach Curry by drinking and using cocaine. I hated the empty feelings of worthlessness I felt now that my football career was cut short. When my career didn't work out, I felt like a failure because my identity had always been wrapped up in who I was as a football player. I felt like I had let my family down. I was a has-been, a nobody. I was confused and miserable because the thing that had caused me such great joy was now the same thing that caused me such grave sorrow. Without football, I thought my life was over. The scandal that was brought about by my reporting that money had been given to me while playing football at Alabama was my way to fight back. It was my revenge on the system. I didn't see how I had allowed my anger at others to take me there, to take me to the epitome of my anger.

Vengeance is not ours to take. Attempting to avenge myself took me down the path of destruction, the likes of which I had never seen nor heard of. It brought me to the streets of the abyss, an empty bottomless pit of darkness and evil. I was destroying myself. I was destroying my family. I was destroying my destiny. I was, not God, nor other people. I had eaten out of garbage cans with the rats, slept in the dark alleys with the dead, and walked what seemed like thousands of miles begging for food as if I were a zombie. I was tired. I was tired of living in the pigsty and eating pig slop. I came to myself. I didn't want to be angry anymore. It was finally dawning on me the cost of my resentment. I tried to stop being angry. I honestly believed I could stop. I could overcome this anger that had festered until it had become irrational. I had simply been fooling myself by just trying to hope in positive thinking. I said to myself, "You are strong enough to bounce back from being hurt." But I wasn't. After so many years of nursing it, I couldn't just stop being angry on my own. I tried to stop, but I failed each time. I finally admitted, "I can't, but God can. Lord, help me. I want to go home. I want to stop being angry." I didn't know how, but I didn't have to know, God knew.

Gene Jelks

I received a call from Walter Lewis. He is a good Christian man, who I greatly admire. He talked to me for thirty minutes. During our conversation, he told me that I should go and see Coach Curry. He said, "You know, I'm neutral in all this Gene. I don't keep up with the news about you. I care about you and I know your family; they are good Christian people. You are still bitter, Gene, and until you go and talk with Coach Curry about how you feel and what you thought he did to you, you're still going to be bitter and your blessing will be cut off and put on hold." I knew he was telling me the truth. I knew it came straight from God, because deep down, I knew this too. I just had to get past the bitterness and anger. After listening to Walter talk on and on about Coach Curry, I was tired of hearing his name, so I reached down deep inside my soul and said out of anger, "Okay, Walter, I will go see him!" I thought I was finished and that would shut him up, so I made an excuse and said, "I don't know how to get in touch with the coach, and I certainly don't know where the guy is." Walter, knowing I was making excuses gave me the information. I knew it was God and that same day, in 2011, I started searching for Coach Curry. I was broke, but I still tried to keep my promise. I went to the Georgia State weight room and spoke to the strength coach. I said, "Hello, my name is Gene Jelks, and I am looking for Coach Curry." He looked at me and said, "I know who you are. I watched you play on television. You were a great football player." Humbled, I said, "Thanks, Coach." He gave me directions to the Georgia State football facility. I walked five miles to the facility and saw a lady in the parking lot. I asked her if she knew where Coach Curry was. She told me to just go to the door and knock; someone would come to the door. I knocked, and a man came to the door and asked, "Can I help you?" I said, "Yes. Do you know if Coach Curry is here?" He said, "He is in a football meeting with his staff." I wrote a note and asked the man if he would give the note to him. He took it and left. I walked off, headed to the Marta train station. Five minutes later, Coach Curry called me and asked me if I could come back to meet with him. I said, "Sure!"

Walking Across The Bridge

He was waiting for me in the parking lot. As I walked up to him, I had mixed emotions. We hugged each other and went to the football conference room and sat down. We began to talk. I said, "I have something on my mind that I want to say." He said, "What is it?" I said, "You know I am homeless and I sleep under a bridge close to your office by Underground Atlanta." He said, "I didn't know this, Gene. I'm sorry!" I continued to tell him that I had been angry with him for nineteen years because he moved me from the starting running back position to defensive back. I asked him, "Why did you move me?" He said, "I had two great running backs and I did not know what to do with both of you. I didn't know you were that sensitive." I started crying. That's when I told him, "You cost me my dream." He said, "I owe you that much to listen to you." We continued to talk for a while, and then we parted on good terms. It was the beginning of my healing and breakthrough.

I realized I had made a mistake when I lashed out in anger, causing people who once were my friends to turn against my family and me. The day I agreed with the man who showed up at my house so long ago, which led to the scandal, was the day I unwittingly ruined my life. Because of that decision, I was blackballed, had death threats and was forced from the life I had known. I felt as if I had been quarantined on a deserted island, far away from everyone and everything I had ever loved. When I saw my name splattered all over the news media and realized many of these stations were telecast all over the country, I realized my mistake, but it was too late. In the midst of my isolation, I asked God to forgive me for what I did against Him, to my family, to my friends, the Alabama brotherhood football program, the University of Alabama, the fans, and associates, and anyone else I hurt. I went to everyone who I had caused pain and hurt and tried to make amends with them. I asked all of them to forgive me for the embarrassment and harm I'd caused them. Many people forgave me; some didn't, not yet anyway. I have to live with that because I don't know what I would have done if the shoe were on the other foot. We have all sinned and come short of the glory of God. The day that I spoke with Coach Curry was the day I was set free from bondage. It felt good. I still have resentment toward him, yet I knew that I was close to the end of the bridge. I knew that God was still working in and on me while showing me His love and mercy. My Father God, like the father in the story of the prodigal son, embraced me, and said, "Welcome back, son."

Chapter 10
Going Home

Dorothy said it best when she said, "There's no place like home." Like the son in the prodigal story, I HIT ROCK BOTTOM. The son spent all his money and ended up in the pigpen eating what others had thrown out, what they no longer wanted and left for the pigs to eat. I have experienced those things, foraging for leftover food with the animals. Life can be hard and my life has been hard going from being famous and cheered one day, to being humbled and broken the next. Psalm 34:18 says, *"The LORD is nigh unto them that are of a broken heart; and saveth such as be of a contrite spirit."* That's the King James Version; however, the New Living Translation makes it a little clearer, *"The LORD is close to the brokenhearted; he rescues those whose spirits are crushed."*

My heart was broken and my spirit was crushed. I cried out to the Lord and He heard my cry. Nothing more is required when out of true desperation we cry to Him because we realize we can do nothing in our own strength. We must call on the only One who can truly help. This is where true humility meets true godliness. It was at this moment that I realized I have nothing, and all the self-confidence I thought I had was gone. My heart was aching, my soul was hurting and my mind had gone blank. The drugs, the women, the fame, the money, the power, the abilities, the gifts and the education meant nothing. I had it all, and I lost it all. Through rebellion, heartache, pain, suffering, almost being killed, and a heart attack, I realized the Lord was with me all along, even though I had stopped praying and serving Him. I had been searching for Him the whole time, only I didn't know it. I needed Him to fill that place that only He can fill. "Speak, Lord, for your prodigal child is finally listening." When I finally sat still, that's when I began to hear Him.

God was pushing me to go back home to Alabama. He was transitioning me because He knew Alabama was where my heart was, even though I made a mistake. I was born and raised in Gadsden. I am proud to be from the City of Champions. Alabama is where I belong. He knew I had suffered and had been homeless long enough. I made it only because of His grace and mercy. When I reflect on my past struggles and all my challenges, I can't thank Him enough for His mercy and protection. I still didn't know how to get back to Alabama and what to do, because even though I knew this in my heart, I was still scared to face some things. I was still frightened for my life. But God was with me and He was leading me.

It was a bright hot summer day in Georgia; outside the sweltering heat scorched and wilted nearly everything. I was feeling down, the gloom had set in again. I just started walking down a rural street with my head bowed, searching for answers. My feet were hot and burning, and sweat was pouring down my body, soaking my clothes. I had no money to even buy a bottle of water, feeling dehydrated, I stopped by a hospital and sat on the street guardrail to rest. I prayed to God for help, "Lord, help me. I need a ride because it's hot. I feel too weak to walk out here anymore." Twenty minutes later a white man pulled up and asked me if I needed a ride. Though I had prayed for help, I said, "No, I don't know you." He said, "It's hot and you look as if you could use a ride." I was afraid and caution made me refuse his offer. He convinced me he was picking up his son at the bus stop. I just looked at him and one minute later the bus pulled up twenty yards from where I was sitting and his son came to the car, so

I got in. I was convinced then that he was trying to help me without some kind of catch. As I sat in the car, the cool air blew in my face and it wasn't long until I felt better, restored. He introduced me to his son. He asked me where I lived. I was too embarrassed to tell him I was homeless, so I told him to just drop me off up the road at the gated town houses. When he pulled up to the gate, he started talking about the Word of God and encouraging me to be strong and allow God to guide me out of my troubles. I got out of the car and said, "Thank you, sir, for the ride." I believe he was an angel sent by God. The revelation I got from this events was that God was letting me know He was with me the entire time.

In April of 2011, Alabama was struck by a violet EF4 multiple-vortex tornado. It devastated parts of the cities of Birmingham and Tuscaloosa. One morning I was home alone feeling disheartened about the tornado, and my life, so I called a minister to talk about how depressed I was becoming. As I was talking to him about my situation, the minister suggested I take a walk and talk to God. I brushed my teeth, put on some clothes and off I went, walking. I walked three miles across a road creek bridge. I stopped and stared at the muddy creek water while listening to the sound of God's creation, the water running between the rocks. It was a beautiful sound to my ears. I began to go deep in my soul, talking to God. As I walked to my daughter's home, a soft voice spoke to me, "Walking across the bridge." This is the title God gave me for this book. What an amazing God we serve. I didn't write this book right away because I was still homeless. It would be years later when I would finally be able to write the book. I knew the Lord was guiding me to go back home to Gadsden, but my heart was heavy and uncertain. I was not sure if I would ever be accepted back in Alabama.

Another evening I went for a jog. Jogging was my time for solace and peace. It was when I could hear the Voice of God. While jogging, it began to rain. I jogged to a closed fruit stand and stood under its tent until the rain stopped. It was under the tent, in the pouring rain that I experienced a peace, the peace I had been searching for. I was once again thinking about the tornado that struck down in T-Town. I longed to go back and help the city clean up the aftermath. I never thought about going back before, but this time, I knew in my heart, it was what I needed to do, and where I belonged. It was then I knew I was going home. I just didn't know how. But God knew. When the rain stopped, I walked the rest of the way back to my daughter's house. It was a three-mile peaceful journey.

Out of nowhere, I got a call from Noel Humphrey, who was a preacher. He suggested that I go with him to Tuscaloosa, or T-town, as it is commonly called by the locals. He had to preach at a church revival and he thought it would be a good idea if I went. I froze for a minute. Finally I said, "Sure", but I was not sure if it would be a good idea for me to show up in Tuscaloosa after my part in the investigation at Alabama. After I hung up with the preacher, I told myself, I can do this, just be brave and hope for the best. I had nothing to lose. I prayed to God about it and I told God I went through a tornado in my life, but nothing like the tornado that touched down in the state and the devastation that happened in Tuscaloosa. I was trying to build up the courage to go back and help out the tornado victims. God told me to quietly go back. Humphrey picked me up, and off to Tuscaloosa we went. When we arrived at the FEMA site in North Port to volunteer, there was a newspaper reporter waiting to interview me. I was nervous because I hadn't talked to a reporter from Alabama in almost nineteen years. I certainly didn't want to talk about the Alabama scandal; I was trying to forget about the whole painful ordeal. I was trying to let that go. I did the interview and then I went to volunteer, helping people who were receiving the donation of clothes at the door, and then taking the clothes to the proper stations. People were curious and some were watching my every move. Some were talking and saying, "He just saw an opportunity." It was not like that at all. I went to do what God said to do. I kept quiet. I trusted Him without wavering. I volunteered all day until it was time to go back to our hotel. I talked to some Bama fans I knew, and they said welcome back home, Gene. That was a relief. An Alabama football player took me around the city to see all of the wreckage and damage the tornado had caused. I was speechless at what I saw. There was nothing but a stretch of open field, land and lumber, which used to be homes, scattered on the ground. The trees were ripped from the ground at the roots. We went back to the FEMA location and back to volunteering again. Again, there were people watching me all day to see if I came to get recognition, or if I actually came to volunteer. I stayed focused on working all day, thanking God for his favor for allowing me to be of help, and also for protecting me at all times. A reporter sent me a newspaper article. I was nervous, but opened the sports section and to my surprise saw the headlines, "Silent Salvation". I was shocked because I thought the media was going to write bad things about me being back in T-town. That's when I knew one thing for sure: If God is for you, who can be against you?

That same year, after going back to help with the cleanup after the tornado, I heard rumors that Coach Ray Perkins was having a football reunion in Tuscaloosa. I wanted to go back and be reunited with the "A" Club, the football Lettermen, but I was too scared to just show up at the reunion, so I called my mentor Kerry Goode and talked to him about my situation. He told me that I needed to own up to my mistake and go to the football reunion. I went back to Tuscaloosa and I met with all of the alumni, and for the most part everybody embraced me. I saw Hoss Johnson outside and I ran over to him and jumped up in his arms and started hugging him real tight as if I were a little boy. Johnson is also a Christian mentor who was one of our offensive linemen at Alabama. He's a great man of God. I was nice and kind to everybody and most of the club football Lettermen were nice to me. I even got the chance to see one of my upperclassmen, Chester Bragg. I was a happy man to be back home at Alabama where my college football career started.

Gene Jelks

When the reunion was over, a lot of the former players walked up to Coach Perkins hugging, laughing, talking and taking pictures with him. Feeling a bit nervous, I gently approached Coach and we greeted each other in peace. It was a great feeling. When I was getting out of the car, Bo Jackson slowly drove by and rolled down his car-tinted window and looked at me and smiled. I said, "What's up, Bo? We're going to win again just like old times at Legion field in the 1985 Iron Bowl." Bo chuckled. A sponsor put together a celebrity A-Day alumni charity flag football game in 2011 in Hoover, Alabama for the tornado victims. The game was Alabama vs. Auburn. Alabama won the game by one point. Roll Tide! Some of the Alabama players were not happy that I came and played in the game. It did bother me, but I had to overlook this and realize it takes time for some people. I couldn't focus on that, but the thing that really mattered. I did what I thought was best for me. I thought time had healed the old wounds, but I guess I was wrong. I ignored the comments and enjoyed reuniting with my brotherhood. After the game, both schools went out to socialize and we all had a good time. Chris Goode made sure that I was all right. God knew I needed to socialize with my friends because I had been gone for nineteen years and I missed them.

After the football game, and seeing all the guys, going back to Atlanta, where I was living in between places, I knew I didn't want to be homeless again. I was still with my daughter off and on. She was asking me what I wanted to do, because she and her fiancé were making plans for their lives. She didn't want me back on the streets, so she told me that her mother, who had been my girlfriend long ago, wanted me to move in with her so I could have a stable place to live. I really didn't think it was a good idea, but not wanting to go back to the streets or a shelter, I did move in with her mother. Things didn't work out, and I moved out. We will always have a precious daughter together, and for that I am very grateful, and because of this, she will always have a special place in my heart. However, I learned, you can't move backward, when God wants you to move forward.

Walking Across The Bridge

With me moving out and trying to make it on my own, things weren't working out the way I had hoped. I was at a crossroad. My daughter had moved on with her life. I was trying to make it on my own, and I didn't want to be a burden on her and her fiancé. She had helped me a lot already, but I was the parent and she was the child. It was time to reverse roles. So just thinking and praying, contemplating everything, I finally knew what I had to do. Sitting by the picnic area outside of my daughter's mother's apartment complex, I called my cousin Gene Lett to send me a one-way bus ticket to Gadsden.

I really thought before I called my cousin that I could find a job to pay rent for an apartment, but God kept closing doors. A neighbor helped me move in a rooming house for a week. I didn't have any money to pay next week's rent so I called Siran Stacy and he sent me $300. But that wouldn't last forever; I still had to have money for rent later. I prayed to God to help me make the right decision about whether to stay in Atlanta or go back to Gadsden. I talked with several God-fearing people and they gave me some great advice. Just to be sure and to confirm what they told me, I called my friend Bishop Steve Smith. I told him what the other people said and that my heart was heavy. I was burdened with the challenge of having the money to pay my rent, but couldn't find a job. He told me that it's not worth all the challenges and hardship I had to face. He said, "You need to come back home where people love you and maybe God has a blessing for you here." When he said this, it was like a burden was lifted off me and it felt like confirmation. I picked up the bus ticket at Greyhound and could not wait to board. I knew there weren't many opportunities in Gadsden, but all I wanted was some peace. In the end, it was the best move I had made in a long time.

The Long Walk Home
(The End of the Bridge)

Chapter 11
Grace Restored

Riding that Greyhound bus back to Gadsden in 2011, my mind went a hundred miles a minute with thoughts in my head about what I was going to encounter when I reached my destination. Was I going to get a hero's welcome from my family and friends, or would people only remember me for the bad things I had done? It was hard for me going back home, and many times on that short trip back to Gadsden, I wanted to run, to escape like I had in the past. But something kept me from running this time. It wasn't me, because if it were left up to me, I would run. It was the grace of God within me that kept me from running. It was His love, His mercy, and His peace. Although I didn't know what to expect when I reached Gadsden, I knew that God was with me, and if He is with you, who and what can be against you? I just knew that I was sick and tired of living like I had been living. I was tired of being alone and stressed out.

I got a call from Coach Ray Perkins one Sunday before I left. He said he had read an article online which reported that I was once homeless. I told him that it was true. He then asked me if I was okay. I replied, "Things are getting better." He encouraged me to do the right thing. He said, "Remember, you are still the same guy I recruited when you were in high school. You still have a good heart, and everyone knows this." I said, "Thank you, Coach." He said, "I love you." I said, "I love you too." That was a call I needed. It helped me. I knew it was God telling me, "I have you. Don't worry." Everyone said the same thing, but since I was on the other side, it was hard to comprehend, but that phone call from Coach Perkins brought everything into perspective.

I knew everything my family, friends and Coach Perkins were saying to me was the truth. Their words were confirmation from God; yet, would their encouraging words suffice for the long road I was traveling? When I spoke to them, my confidence was high, my courage was intact, but on that Greyhound, the closer I got to Gadsden, my destination, my confidence and my courage started to waiver. Though many of my friends and family members said I needed to come back home, I was fully aware that it's always easier for others to say what they would do, when they don't have to do it. When I was traveling down that road, even though I knew the truth, I knew the answer, there were doubts, there were fears, and there were "what if's," because, in all honesty, I just didn't know. I didn't know what to expect, and I was a little scared of the unknown.

I had mixed emotions when I finally arrived in Gadsden. I was happy I was home, but in low spirits at the same time because I still didn't feel free from the sports scandal. Taking a deep breath, I picked up my bags and headed for home. My family's house was only one block from the bus station, so with my suitcase and carry-on bag in my hands, I walked to the house where I had lived as a child, the house that was always filled with love. I had only happy memories of love, warmth and peace while living there. When I approached the house, I hesitated. I was no longer the man I was then when I had left for college so long ago. I had changed. Life and my circumstances had changed me. I wasn't that innocent young man anymore who saw the world through rose-colored glasses. I was no longer that man who believed that if I did what was right, everything would be okay. I had learned the hard way that everything doesn't always work out as planned. Often in life, we travel roads that aren't paved; they are dirt roads, muddy roads. And, everyone knows that on dirt roads people get dirty. However, it was my life. Some things that happened were my fault, and some things that happened weren't. Even though it wasn't what I had planned for myself, I learned a lot, and most importantly, I had grown up, for the mere fact that I had no other choice. The choice was either to stay where I was and die or grow and live. I chose to grow and live. The first step in my growth was to go home and face the unknown.

When I walked into the house and saw my mother, I went over to her and gave her a big, long hug and a kiss. It felt good to hear her heartbeat, to feel her warmth and love and enjoy just the familiar smell of her. I was finally home. I talked to my mother for a while and couldn't wait to eat a good, home-cooked meal, take a shower and go to sleep in a warm, clean bed. The first months were easy for me. My mother had back surgery so the first three months I cared for her. I would help her put clean bandages on her back, take her to the doctor, take her to therapy, cook her meals and assist her at home with whatever was needed. I visited her when she was in rehab. When she was strong enough to walk and do for herself, I started going back to church and attending a weekly Bible study.

Once my mother was doing better, and I started going to church, I knew it was time for me to get a job. I called my former boss at Big Lots to see if she would rehire me. She was no longer with the company, but I still filled out the application. I went to Walmart and filled out an application. Three weeks later, Walmart's Human Resources Department called me for an interview. I passed two interviews and they told me what was available. I was desperate for employment. I told the supervisor that I would take an entry-level position as an associate. He said someone would call me. No one called me back, so I kept calling human resources to follow up about the position, but no one would give me a straight answer. I told my mother I was becoming frustrated, and my patience was growing thin. As usual, she was encouraging and said, "You have to be patient. Something will come through for you." I mostly stayed in the house watching television. One Monday morning I decided to check with several temporary employment agencies. I filled out applications and waited, hoping and praying someone would call me for a job. An agency finally did. My mother informed me that a temp agency called me about a job. I got excited and ran to the phone and called them back. The agent told me that KTH Production had an opening. I drove to the temp agency and took a drug test, passed it, and they gave me instructions about where and when I had to go to orientation in Centre, Alabama, about thirty miles from Gadsden. I worked at KTH Production for a year. It felt good having a job. Every week when I got paid I would give my mother money to help with bills. After nineteen years of being unemployed, I now had a steady income. It felt good.

Helping my mother recover from back surgery helped me too. I didn't have to think about a lot of things. I didn't want to think about, or go anywhere where I would have to see people. I didn't have to answer to anyone about my past. But as my mother grew stronger, and I started attending church and working, I knew that I would have to revisit and deal with the past. After all, Gadsden was a small community and everyone, black and white, knew each other or knew each other's relatives. It was always, "Aren't you so and so's boy?" The South is known for its hospitality, courtesy, and manners. When asked these questions, we would respond with, "Yes, sir" or "Yes, ma'am", especially if the person we are addressing is elderly, regardless of the color of the skin. It's the Southern way. I had to face people who I thought would welcome me back into their bosom with open arms, or at least, do so because of the grace they had received from God. Some did, and some didn't. Regarding some of the ones who didn't, I was surprised at their snubs. I felt bad because no matter what I had done in the past, I was still the "Jelks" boy that they knew growing up. It was very hard for me when some of the blacks in my community shunned me. I attempted to make amends with some of them, but they didn't accept my apology. I expected this from other people, but not from my community. When this happened, I walked away in dismay and never looked back or crossed their paths again.

I called an Alabama Alumni booster and made amends with him. He accepted my apology and he forgave me. As I learned to forgive myself, I was becoming free in my spirit and I began to heal from holding those burdens inside for so many years. Time went on, and people reacted in many different ways. Some would speak while some would stare and some would call me a snitch. Some would say, "That's Gene Jelks, an Alabama legend. He was a running back, and boy, was he fast!" There were still others who would have nothing to do with me. It was those individuals who hurt me the most. They were the ones who always focused on what I did, and not what I was becoming. It's funny because they would base their opinions on something I did to myself, and my circle, and not what I did to them. They held onto my past mistake while the ones who were affected by my actions forgave me. In the end, it was me who suffered, not the people who couldn't get past what I did. Their life went on; my life took a dark turn down a path of almost no return.

For this reason, the people who wouldn't let me forget my past, it was difficult for me to adjust to living in Gadsden. I had learned to survive living on the streets for so long and had been used to being let down when I didn't have a place to live, that in my self-defense, I just became numb from everything. Living on the streets didn't hurt me, particularly during the day, because I was just surviving, not living. However, when I came back home, to the world that I had left behind, my world full of friends and family, it was survival for me too. Yet this was a different kind of survival. Not the way I had to survive as a homeless person, but just to survive around people who still remembered my past, and wouldn't let it go. It took me a while to adjust to having a safe environment, a stable home to live in, food on the table, and a clean, warm bed to sleep in, because even though I had all the comforts of home, in my mind, I still was reliving my past. I was still allowing a few people's snubs and opinions to keep me in bondage. It took me four years of being back home to overcome my shame, guilt, and fear. I overcame with the help of God, my family and friends, and their love for me. People told me they still loved me, and all was forgiven. We all make mistakes in life, but since I had been a local celebrity and my mistake was made public on TV and in the newspapers, it caused my recovery to be a little harder and slower. Being confident in the love of my family and friends helped me to heal and rest assured that I was safe again. It was in these moments I learned about God's grace.

Every day, we walk in God's grace and mercy. Grace is given to us freely; we cannot earn it, buy it, sell it or produce it. Grace is given to the rich, as well as to the poor. The Lord gives it to all, black and white, Hispanic, Asians, Jews and Gentiles. Grace is God's unmerited favor. Grace is God giving us something we do not deserve. God gives it to us because He loves us. Mercy is God withholding judgment or evil that we deserve; grace is God blessing me in spite of my sins or wrongdoings. Grace justifies me. Grace doesn't give me what I deserve, but what I do not deserve. Because of God's mercy, I do not receive the judgment of God against my sins; because of God's grace, I receive eternal life and a promise of Heaven, though I do not deserve them. Both mercy and grace come to me through the Lord Jesus Christ.

It was grace that kept me from dying in the wilderness when I was homeless. It was grace that kept me from overdosing on drugs. It was grace that kept my heart beating when I had a heart attack. I had to learn that through it all, God's grace kept me even when I didn't want to be kept, or when I didn't know what to do. There were people who shunned me, talked about me, and never forgot what I did. Yes, I already stated that I did it. I took the money while playing at Alabama, and later reported it. I made the mistake. I take full responsibility for it though I severely regretted my action; however, I can't turn back time. I can't fix the damage, the pain or the suffering, but God's grace can and did. We forget that we all fall short of perfection. No one is perfect, and everyone makes mistakes. Whether mistakes are public or private, they are painful. We forget this when the shoe is on the other foot. We forget this when the finger is not pointing at us and at somebody else. We forget this when our issue or struggle is not exposed. We want to blame others for what they did, the hurt they caused, but we fail to blame ourselves for what we did, or the hurt we caused. And I felt that one thing was for certain: No one was hurt more than I was by my mistakes.

I hurt family and friends, and people have hurt me. I had to live with this realization for many years. Sometimes when I think about all that I did, and all the people I hurt, I still cry out to God. It is in those moments, He always tells me, "I have you. My grace is sufficient. Don't worry about what you did; focus on who you belong to and where you are going." I can choose to be forever in bondage by my past, or by what others think of me. Instead, I chose to let God's grace heal me and free me. It was hard in the beginning, especially when I heard the snide remarks, or saw the accusing faces. It was hard when I watched Alabama play football. It was hard when I watched pro football games. However, because God loves me even when I didn't love myself, or when others didn't love me, I was able to hold my head up high and focus on His love and His grace. His grace was enough for me no matter what I faced. It was enough for me no matter what people said. It was enough for me when I didn't know what to do about the remarks or the stares, and when I wanted to run from the guilt, shame and embarrassment. It was enough for me in my pain, my suffering and even in my tears.

Gene Jelks

I learned that grace is a part of God's character. I didn't deserve it, but He loves me so, He gives it to me. He didn't judge me. He didn't condemn me. He welcomed me in His arms, He held me, and comforted me. He didn't tell me what I did; He didn't keep bringing up my past. He restored me. He made me feel like Gene Jelks again. He made me feel whole again. It was hard when I fell. It was hard when I was caught up in sin, or a struggle. People looked at me differently. They judged and condemned me. It's hard to bounce back from this. I know, because I almost didn't. If I had allowed the remarks or the stares to get to me, I probably would still be homeless, strung out on drugs, or worse, dead. Again, I am not saying I wasn't wrong. I admitted my wrongdoing. I thank God that those individuals who condemned and judged me didn't have a role in my being forgiven and restored.

God graced me with so many wonderful people who loved me, and helped me. They never looked at, or focused on, what I did. They always focused on the love of God, and my wholeness as a person. In God's eyes, I am worth fighting for. Just as my parents had always told me so many years ago, I am special; I'm not a throwaway or a has-been. I'm a force to be reckoned with. It's His grace that keeps and restores me and will continue to keep and restore me. Not because I deserve it, but because He loves me and that is what grace is all about. We tend to forget that everyone, at least, some time in their lives, more than once, needs God's grace and mercy. It was His grace that allowed me to make it those four years living in Gadsden, and it will be His grace that will continue to uphold me.

In retrospect, in the past, my family had to deal with my anger and my bad behavior because I had not let go of my hurt. My family had gotten to the point that they did not know who I was anymore. This affected them greatly. They hurt because it was unbearable for them not knowing how I would act from day to day. I regret putting my family through hell. It's something I am not proud of because I love them so much. I had anger that I could not explain or control. When I went home, I knew I had to face my demons, my actions and my past. I admitted to my mother, family and friends that I messed up. I was to blame for my mess. I owned up to my faults. I didn't handle the situation with Alabama correctly. I was sorry I put them through the hurt, shame and disgrace. I ran on self-will, pride and arrogance, but like the prodigal son in Luke 15, I was home to stay. No more running. I sinned against God, and them, and because of this I felt I wasn't worthy to be called their son, their family member, or their friend. Time spanked me and spanked me good.

My family listened quietly and patiently, and then, just like the father with the son, with tears in their eyes, they embraced me with welcome and open arms, kissing and hugging me, telling me they loved me, and yes, I was still theirs. I was still Gene Jelks from Gadsden, Alabama. For the first time in a very long time, I knew I was right where God wanted me to be… home. I was at the final steps of the bridge. My journey was about to end.

Chapter 12
Forgiveness is Not an Option

Letting go and forgiving others and myself was probably the hardest part of my walk. And I must confess, it was a long, slow process. In order for God to heal me and for me to grow, I had to forgive. It wasn't an option. For the past nineteen years, I lived with the shame, guilt, and embarrassment of what I did to my family, my friends and my community. I wasn't raised to be a "bad boy." I was raised in a good Christian environment, with two parents who loved, nurtured and provided for me. My siblings and I were blessed. We may not have had much, but we didn't feel poor because there was so much love around us. I was raised in church. The pastor knew my name. He prayed for me. My father taught me values. He taught me how to work and provide for my family. He taught me how to love a woman by the way he loved my mother. My father taught me how to respect the law, my elders and others who had authority over me. My mother taught me how to love a man by the way she loved my father. My mother taught me manners, hospitality and how to treat people the way I wanted to be treated. They were not perfect, but they were perfect in my eyes.

People often wondered, and some even asked, how did I get to that place? How did I become homeless? To be honest, I can't really explain exactly what happened. I can't explain because I really don't know. No one wakes up one morning and says, "Today, I am going to be homeless. Today, I will be living on the streets, begging for food, and sleeping in the gutters." No. We say, "Today, I will get that job." "I will get my degree." "I will become somebody." Being homeless just happens, and for me, that's what happened. One day, I was in a warm bed, the next day I was living on the streets. As time went by, it became my way of life, my normal everyday reality. It became too easy to accept that way of life, because in my mind, it was all an illusion. It was my life, even though it was hard. You cannot judge or condemn me, because we all have moments when insanity takes over our sanity. Some people may handle it differently, but we all have come to this point in our lives. That's why now I tell people, never say what you will or will not do because you'll never know where your situation or circumstance will take you. You don't always know what you would do until you are faced with the same facts.

I was filled with guilt, shame, embarrassment, and most of all, un-forgiveness. I couldn't get over the fact that I had hurt so many people who had loved me unconditionally. I allowed my anger and un-forgiveness to get the best of me. I was angry at what I perceived others did to me, and some of them did do me wrong; however, what they did was on them. It was still no excuse for me to refuse to forgive. My anger turned into bitterness. In my irrational mind, it was them and not me who caused me so much pain, who took away my destiny, and who caused me to do what I did. They were the ones who made me embarrass my family and friends. They caused all the unhappiness in my life.

The un-forgiveness turned to into anger and the anger flared up, and the result was bitterness of the heart. It was them that made the decision over my life that I had no control over. I admit to nursing the anger and allowing it to turn to bitterness. I felt justified being furious, because those decisions did not affect other people as they had me and my future. I didn't know this then, but if I had trusted God, He would have taken that anger and replaced it with liberating love. He would have still given me a wonderful life, football or no football. Learning this was hard but it was a part of my growing up. Sometimes it's true that youth is wasted on the young.

The un-forgiveness that rooted in my heart caused me grief, isolation, and it caused me nineteen years of my life. That's what un-forgiveness does. It keeps us from moving forward from the event, the hurt or pain. We become stagnant, unproductive, and lifeless. We become prisoners of our own minds and souls. My prison was being homeless and for a while, it was anger, and then it was being addicted to alcohol and drugs. Countless others' prisons are also alcohol and drugs, but that isn't all a person's prison can be. It can be overeating, pornography, racism, hatred and a million other vices. When we allow un-forgiveness to continue its dark path of destruction, we experience depression, stress, or anxiety, which, if we are not careful, can cause life-threatening illnesses, as it did for me, when I suffered a heart attack. All of these things can be a result of un-forgiveness; however, the number one thing un-forgiveness does is it alienates us from God. A heart can be so full of anger, self-pity and bitterness, that God's love cannot penetrate its core because steel walls have been built around it. We say, "I'm okay. I got this." But we don't. I know, because I didn't.

It's hard to forgive, especially when we feel we are the victim. We were betrayed or wronged, and it's true, we were. I believe I stayed homeless for those many years because I didn't want to believe I was wrong in some ways too. I just focused on what they did to me and not what I did to others. I didn't want to admit it and say, "Lord, it's me, not them." I was in fear of losing my ground, my right to say it was them and not me. What would I do if I did not blame others anymore? The answer to that would have been to point the finger at me, and truthfully, that is a hard thing to do and accept. Because then I would have to admit all the wandering, the lost years, the pain and loneliness, were not the other guy's fault, but my own. To admit I could have saved myself so much grief was hard, if not downright impossible for me to bear, for a long, long time. My anger and my self-righteousness produced the adrenaline that kept me going. It fed my anger and kept me bound. The more I thought about that day when my position was switched, the angrier I would become, which goes to show how dwelling on painful things others have done to us, disappointments, insults or problems only results in more pain. Though we may not realize it, this pain is self-inflicted.

I was in fear that I would not be able to save face; I would lose my power and control. I was considered small as a running back; I was. However, my speed and agility made up for my size. Many would say I was too small to be a football player, let alone play for Alabama and the pros. I proved all of them wrong. In my un-forgiveness, I kept thinking those thoughts of what people said about me. I believed in my rational-irrational thinking that those comments were one of the connecting factors to be upset about when my position was switched. It caused me to want to prove that I was the man for the job, and that my size didn't matter. That's how the enemy plays with our mind, because that little thought, became a seed, along with the other seeds, and as a result, un-forgiveness grew in my heart.

In 1 John 1:9, it says, "If we confess our sins, he is faithful and just to forgive us of our sins and to cleanse us from all unrighteousness." I knew that to be free, I had to forgive myself and forgive everyone else. I had to release myself and others so I could live again. I couldn't forgive through my strength; I had to do it through God's strength. I had to allow Him to show me how to forgive myself and others. I had to have faith in Him that He would do it because to be honest, it's not easy. Our natural instinct, man's basic selfishness is to refuse to forgive and to get even for the wrong, the betrayal, and in some cases the perceived wrong. That's when I cried out to the Lord in distress, and he heard my cry and started me on the path to healing and forgiveness (Psalm 120:1).

The first encounter I had in learning to forgive was in 2007. I went to a ministry outreach event. The minister told us that God forgives His children and we must ask Him for forgiveness for ourselves and to forgive others. When we ask for this with a sincere heart, He pours His love into us until we can learn to love ourselves again. Those words stuck with me that day. I will never forget those words because my healing and breakthrough were taking place. I had to learn how to let go of negative feelings and turn them into positive feelings. I had to learn how to change my attitude about how I once viewed the beautiful world that God created and all things that were good. For many years I was numb and angry; however, when I learned to forgive, I learned not to beat myself up anymore and not to dwell on my mistakes. I began to read the Bible passages concerning forgiveness. I put the word of God in the place of all my bad thoughts. Little by little, I started to see a change. I began to smile again. When I began forgiving myself and others, my family and friends started noticing the change. As a result, my family started forgiving me for what happened. We conducted an intervention, a group session where I told them how I felt and asked them for forgiveness. They responded with comments about how they were affected by the scandal, and how they felt about it. I began to cry hearing how my actions had hurt my family, but it was a relief to have it out in the open. We were all healing now. After our group discussion, we began to hug each other with tears streaming down our faces. Later, we went over to my aunt's house to eat and fellowship. It was a blessed day! My family told me that they were going to help me recover and said for me to leave all the bad things in the past and move forward with my life. They all said, "You have a family who loves you, so you are blessed more than a lot of other people." I knew then my road to forgiveness and restoration was certain.

Gene Jelks

Reconciliation was important to me. I had to earn the trust of my family, friends, associates and the brotherhood at Alabama. That trust was broken by the sports scandal I had caused. I remember being nervous and building up my courage to call Dr. Gary White at the University of Alabama to ask for his forgiveness. We talked, and he forgave me because he is a Christian. We were on friendly terms now. That's the kind of God we serve, the God who is written about in the first chapter of Ephesians. I felt as if a ton of bricks had been lifted off me. I was ashamed to see some of my friends again, but I had to face the music to reconnect with them. It was easier than what I had feared, the scenario that had replayed itself over and over in my head. They forgave me and we ended up talking about Jesus and how good He is. Many of them prayed for me. Look at God! It was a happy feeling reconciling with family and friends. I had missed a lot in those years, not seeing them on a regular basis, especially during the holidays when we would all get together. I had spent many years running with the football; I had also lost many years running away. No more running. Unfortunately, some of the Alabama players did not want to reconnect with me. I understood completely. I have to live with their rejection because I did hurt many of them. I pray that one day they will find it in their heart to forgive me. I have hope because forgiveness is a process. We all must remember that the Bible says all have sinned and come short of the glory of God.

Gratitude overwhelmed me for my family and friends who had forgiven me and welcomed me back into their lives, back into the life I used to live with them. My mother spent many evenings discussing forgiveness with me. Reverend Anthony C. Jelks, my brother, would encourage me to keep moving forward and stop looking back to the past and not to get weary in well-doing. He would tell me, "Stop worrying!" And I would respond to him with, "I love you, boy!" Minister Nathaniel White held a Bible study with me every Tuesday and afterward he would take me out to eat for lunch. Coach Ray Perkins told me to forgive and do the right things in life, to go back to being that guy he knew when he recruited me for Alabama. Bishop Steve Smith shared the word with me about forgiveness. Bishop Walter "Tang" Smith gave me a long lecture about forgiveness. Kerry Goode talked to me about facing my mistakes and to forgive and move forward. Hoss Johnson called me and started preaching about forgiveness. He said, "Some people will forgive and some won't. Don't worry about the ones who won't. Just pray for them." Brother John Saddler would text me Bible verses about forgiveness. Smoke Hodge would talk with me on the phone and encourage me to stay focused and refuse to let people get under my skin because I had made mistakes. He told me to just serve the Lord and He would bless me. Sam Bryant talked with me on the phone. He said, "Don't worry about anything, just tell people you are sorry and then it's no longer on you, it's on them to forgive." Dr. Michael Wesley Sr. worked with me on how to forgive, and told me that practicing forgiveness all the time helped us to stay Christ-like. He encouraged me to trust God and let Him guide and lead me. He advised me to stop being angry and go out and live the life God intended me to live, to allow God to bless me and serve others for His Kingdom.

The miracle happened in the year 2011 when I listened to God's instruction and went back home. From that point, I was able to learn how to forgive. I have forgiven others and have gone to those whom I offended personally and received forgiveness, so that God could unlock my blessings. Today, I concentrate on staying free as I keep moving forward, focusing on my next assignment and sowing seeds to others to be a blessing. I live and let live. I stay in my lane! I had to repent of my past sins so that God could clean my plate. When I read in the Bible that Jesus said we have to forgive others of their sins against us, and if we don't forgive them, then the Heavenly Father does not forgive us of our sins, it blew my mind. God cannot lie, so I had to forgive others and move on to the next play.

Gene Jelks

All in all, forgiveness is a choice we make. It's through a decision of our will, motivated by obedience to God and His word and His love. We must trust God to do the complete work in us that needs to be done so true forgiveness will take place. In our human effort, it's not possible, but when we trust and rely on God, we can do all things through Him who strengthens us. When we forgive, we release the prisoner within ourselves. We become free. We loosen our selves. For this reason, forgiveness is not an option; it's necessary.

Chapter 13
The Road to Restoration

The road to forgiveness was a hard and painful process. I still have wounds, and I must admit, sometimes those past hurts would tempt me to digress to my old ways and feelings. It's a process, and though it is a process, it's also a decision, regardless of how I feel. I'm winning more now, and God is truly showing me how to let go of unnecessary things. He is restoring me. And for this, I am grateful. He is not restoring me back to my mistakes or failures, but back to the beginning when He first breathed life into me and gave me a purpose. He is restoring me so I can fulfill my destiny. There is a Bible verse that we forget to reflect on as it relates to our life. Jeremiah 29:11 says *"For I know the thoughts that I think toward you, saith the Lord, thoughts of peace, and not evil, to give you an expected end."* (KJV). In some versions of the Bible, the word, 'thoughts' is translated to 'plans'. More often than we care to admit, we forget about His plans for our lives and go out and do our own thing, make our own plan…we march to our own drumbeat. Unfortunately, sometimes marching to our own drumbeat takes us to another place where we didn't plan on going.

When we think about restoring, or restoration, we tend to focus on the external and not the internal. We say things like, I need to lose weight, so I have to diet and exercise more. How many of us know that if our mind is not made up on losing weight, we will not lose the weight? We will digress back to our old ways, eating the cake and ice cream after a long day at work, or just snacking on chips and dip while sitting down watching television. To lose the weight, we have to look within; we have to focus on the internal because once the internal is fixed, the external will fall in line. The weight will come off. It's the same way with restoring things. We see a raggedy old couch on the side of the road, and say, "Wow, that's a real ugly couch." We see what it is now, what it has become, due to the wear and tear of someone sitting or lying on it day in and day out. We focus on the now. We don't see the beauty of what it used to be, or even what it could be. However, some people who look beyond the exterior see that it still has good springs, the wood and foundation are still durable. They see the possibility of the couch. They take the battered couch home and restore it to its natural beauty, to its original splendor. Sometimes, they even make it better than the original. Now when people see it, they marvel at its beauty, and how elegant it looks. They don't see what it looked like before the restoration process; they just focus on how it looks now. Many times, we miss out on the raggedy old couch because we never look past its potential. Sadly, that's how we do with each other. We see our flaws, our mistakes, our nakedness, our exposure and our shame. We don't give each other time to go in and take a bath, to clean ourselves up. We don't ask for help if we need it to clean ourselves up. We just see each other like we see that raggedy old couch, ugly and worthless, and needing to be thrown away. I'm so thankful that God doesn't see us, or me, that way. He sees us the way He created us, beautifully; our worth is far above rubies. To Him, we are a diamond in the rough; we are in the fire, waiting to be purified.

Restoration is all about restoring us to our original state of being. Healing is one thing, and it's crucial, but we must also restore the damage, the ugliness, and the barrenness. There were ten lepers who came to Jesus for healing. He was the only cure for leprosy, just as He is the only cure for our ailments. Jesus told them to go show themselves to the priest, as their law dictated. Jesus healed ten, yet only one came back and thanked Jesus.

> *"And it came to pass, as he went to Jerusalem, that he passed through the midst of Samaria and Galilee. And as he entered into a certain village, there met him ten men that were lepers, which stood afar off: And they lifted up their voices, and said, Jesus, Master, have mercy on us. And when he saw them, he said unto them, Go shew yourselves unto the priests. And it came to pass, that, as they went, they were cleansed. And one of them, when he saw that he was healed, turned back, and with a loud voice glorified God, And fell down on his face at his feet, giving him thanks: and he was a Samaritan. And Jesus answering said, Were there not ten cleansed? but where are the nine? There are not found that returned to give glory to God, save this stranger. And he said unto him, Arise, go thy way: thy faith hath made thee whole."* Luke 17: 11-19 (KJV).

This man was not only healed; he was restored. Leprosy is a disease that causes the skin to turn white and die; there is damage where the skin has deteriorated. When he was restored, his skin was made right again. His limbs were usable and functional again. God is in the restoration business. He wants us healed, but He goes farther than healing us. He wants us to thrive and be made whole so He can use us. Nobody wants to feel useless. Restoration is all about restoring you to your original state of being. It's restoring the damage, the ugliness, and the barrenness. It's about taking away the pain and hurt, and putting joy and love in their place. It's about fixing the cracked and broken window, by replacing the windows or fixtures on it. It's about making it usable and functional again. God is in the restoration business. He restores the broken heart, the poor in spirit, the mourners, the persecutors, the comfortless, the lonely, deserted, and the forgotten. He restores the ones who lost their way and don't know how to get back home. He restores the muggers, the thieves, the adulterers, the liars, and the murderers. He even restores the ones who made mistakes.

I had to come to myself and look within, to see the man, not with my eyes, but with my heart. Show the man to the man. I had to face the music, or to put it a better way, I had to look in the mirror and face the man who was staring back at me. It's hard to do this, because if you are sincere, you will see the man behind the shield and the mask. You will see the man behind the facade, the persona. You can't hide from this man, no matter how much you want to. For, this is the man God wants to restore you to, the man He created you to be in the first place. In Psalm 23:3 (KJV), it reads. *"He restoreth my soul: he leadeth me in the paths of righteousness for his name's sake."* There were many things God had to restore in me, but two things were of such magnitude that the other things paled in comparison. The first place where I needed help was to finally let go of the scars, hurt and humiliation of being molested. The second place, which took me to the despair of darkness, was the sports scandal.

I had to deal with being molested in order for the healing process to take place. Now, I know, that I used football as an outlet to forget about the sexual abuse the neighbor had done to me. Football subconsciously helped me move forward. When I played the game, I didn't have to remember the shame of being molested. Football wasn't my only outlet; however, it did keep my mind off the incident. Now I tell people if something bad happens to you, or someone does something bad physically to you, you need to talk about it to someone, regardless if it's a parent, a close relative, a trusted friend, a therapist, or whoever. The key is to talk about the incident. A person may never be healed from the traumatic event if he keeps it bottled up inside. It can destroy you, and one will never be whole until it has been dealt with, no matter how successful they appear to be on the outside. In the back of the mind, hidden away in a dark place that no one knows about, it's still there. You can try to pretend it's not there, but know this, every so often, it may be days, weeks or years, but it will resurface with a vengeance. You must deal with it now so it will have no power over you later. Use it as a tool to help other victims and let them know they are not alone. When people mistreat you or do bad things to you, instead of getting angry, pray about it and talk to God. We have to be honest with Him and tell Him our feelings on the matter and by faith forgive them. He will listen and forgive them that trespass against us, and our trespasses against them, yet more importantly, He will restore us.

It took me many years to deal with being molested. It took years for me to tell someone about the offense. As I said before, I just informed my family in 2015. I always thought it didn't matter. I could control it, but little did I know, it did matter, and I couldn't control it. Now, I'm not saying that being molested was the reason I did what I did concerning the University of Alabama. No. However, I am saying that it did play a role in the matter. Why? When I thought about the incident, it would make me think about other things. I would revert to that time in my life and the fact that people said I was too small to play ball all through my life; at the peewee, middle school, high school, and the collegiate and professional levels. Did it happen because the person thought I was too small to defend myself? Like many other people, did he look at my size and decide that I was vulnerable, an easy target? After all, out of all the other kids playing that day, why did he select me?

I never will forget the day I was molested. I was playing outside with my friends. An older boy got my attention and told me he had some candy and if I wanted some to follow him into the woods three houses down from my grandparents' house. I did. He forced himself on me and made me put his private part in my mouth. Afterwards, he frightened me and told me not to tell anyone or else he would kill me. I felt weird, confused and scared all at the same time. My boyhood was violated. I forgave him many years ago because I realized he was a sick individual to do that to me. But sometimes, as I was growing up, I would think about it and when I did, it bothered me, but I knew I had to continue on in life, so I just put it on the backburner in my mind. I kept moving forward with my life. I don't believe it played a role with me having a temper, because I was five years old when I was molested, so I really didn't know the magnitude of what took place. I just knew it was wrong, and that my innocence as a child was stripped from me. I don't believe it affected my football career either; it was just something I had to deal with and face the fact that it happened to me. That's what freed me from committing suicide and being a victim. I did find peace when I faced him again in person. I forgave him and was finally able to move on from that incident.

The other thing I had to face or deal with was the sports scandal. I needed to be restored from this incident too. I won't go into detail about everything. You can read the papers if you want to know about it and what transpired. There are many speculations about what took place, but the bottom line is, I made a poor decision concerning payments made to me during my college days. I was young, angry and foolish! It happened, and it was one of the worst mistakes I ever made; however, I could not undo it. In the end, no one paid for that mistake more than I did. Going forward, I cannot allow it to dictate my life any more than it has already. God graciously restored me back to the place before the scandal, and I'm grateful for this.

As I look back on why I spent all those years running from my mistake instead of being able to man up to my mess, I didn't think that I would get another chance with the Alabama sports family. But God is awesome! In my restoration, He gave me another chance. I thought it was over; instead, it was the total opposite. As I said, I was feeling guilty and full of mixed emotions, yet when I took that trip to Tuscaloosa it was just like old times with the boys. I missed my friends and all the socializing that we used to do in those days. I realized that all those years away from them had caused me feel as if I were an outcast; it had been my doing, but no more. I had faced down my biggest challenge, and that was facing the Alabama brotherhood. They had accepted me, and I felt restored by them. I already knew God had restored me.

During the process of recovery, I took things one day at a time. It took eight years to rebuild my spiritual foundation. I put in the necessary work to gain my character, integrity and good name back. But it was God who helped me recover by using his recovery principles. If I had not been honest with myself and hadn't applied His road map to my life, I would have died in my mess. My goal for the future was to build an outreach ministry to help kids. This is the vision God gave me while in my restoration process.

The Lord is all about restoring people physically, mentally, and spiritually. Whether we are sick with a disease, or struggling emotionally, or separated from God because of sin, He wants to bring us back into a right relationship with Himself. He wants to fill our lives once again with purpose and contentment. He does not want us to fail. He builds us up to win. In fact, He is our number one supporter, advocate, and cheerleader. As the Psalmist says in 23:3, "He restores my soul. He leads me in paths of righteousness for his name's sake." Jesus does not condemn or judge us; He is in the business of building up, not tearing down. He heals and restores. Therefore, we don't have to focus on our past mistakes, failures, or sin. We focus on Jesus and His unfailing love He has for all of us. When we do this, He will take care of the rest. He is not a respecter of people. He did it for me, and He will do it for anybody. Whatever the enemy has tried to take away, God wants to restore it. God wants to make it better than before. God restored me back to my rightful place, in His will. Today, I'm an author, motivational speaker, and have an outreach ministry and work with young people. When God restores, He thoroughly restores!

Gene Jelks

"For your shame ye shall have double; and for confusion they shall rejoice in their portion: therefore in their land they shall possess the double: everlasting joy shall be unto them." Isaiah 61:7
"I will restore to you the years that the locust has eaten..." Joel 2:25 (KJV).

Chapter 14
Giving Back

As a little boy, I always had a passion to help my elders in my community. When I did some yard work or ran errands for the elderly, they would reward me with money or food. I felt as if I had helped someone and accomplished something when I did those good deeds, especially when I got paid! I had missed that period in my life helping others. One day while I was still in my mess, with tears in my eyes and with a sincere heart, I asked God to help me get out of my mess and to save me. I prayed, "Please send one of your people on earth to give me a sign. I will stop running like Jonah. If you save me, I will give everything back to you so you can bless me. I will do your will and help underprivileged children and any others who are in need." Seven days later God answered my prayer and cries to him. He put a minister in my path for one year, and I never looked back. This is why I give back, because God kept His Word. Thus, I am committed to following Jesus and giving back to help underprivileged children. When people ask me how I made it out of my struggle, I tell them it was only God who saved me, only God! I can't explain it because it was Him, not me. If I could explain it, then it would mean I did it. That's how it is with God. He does it, and all the Glory goes to Him, and not us. What an awesome God we serve! My family and so many people helped me and supported my football career. I had so many positive influences in my life growing up. Then

God saved me. Now it was time for me to do His will for my life and give back. Two events in 2011 led me to the vision or my purpose in helping and giving back to my community.

One morning I was sitting in a sunroom. I had just finished praying to God. He began to speak to me in a soft whisper. The Voice said, "Go back to the beginning." I didn't know the meaning of this right away. The Voice gave me some numbers. I still didn't know what the Lord was instructing me to do. However, being led, for whatever reason, I pulled out a calculator and began to balance my bank account. I didn't know how much money I had in my account because I was not very good at balancing my account. The same number the Voice gave me was the same amount in my bank account. I literally dropped the calculator and almost fell out of the chair. I got goose bumps and became a little afraid. I didn't know what was really happening or what that meant. I tried to figure out what the Voice was saying to me. I opened the Bible and my spirit led me to Genesis 1. When I read it, I said, "Okay! Now I know what I missed in my life. I missed the first step in Alabama of doing God's will for my life, to bless a multitude of people."

During that same time when I was hearing the Voice of the Lord, the doors began to close in Atlanta to me. I knew then God was directing me back to Alabama. On impulse, I picked up the phone and got the number to the Gadsden Chamber of Commerce. When I called, an employee answered the phone and I began to tell her about how God had spoken to me to come back to the beginning, and I wanted her to help me bless the children in the city of Gadsden. She did, and the rest of the glory belongs to God. I have found that the key to this life is obeying Him. I was able to raise $1,200 in two days. I held the 1st Annual Citywide Youth Event at Gadsden State Community College for all kids, regardless of their background, ethnicity or their family's social status. I had the city's blessings from the mayor's office; he supported the event for the children. My dad's best friend, my family, my friends, pastors, the police department and even some of the Alabama boosters supported the youth event. Look at God! God is real. God is a loving and forgiving God. I sowed a seed to 126 children on that Saturday morning. People were asking, "What was going on at Gadsden State and what corporation was supporting the children?" I never said a word to people. I just smiled and gave all the glory to God.

My mother and I took some of the money and bought school supplies for 121 children. I had food donated by many sponsors, thanks to Mrs. Donna Patterson, from the Chamber of Commerce. There were Christian rappers, a live DJ from Atlanta, speakers, city councilmen, air jumpers and lots of music. It was 2011, the year I went back to Gadsden. That was the day God protected me, and like He did for the children of Israel, He parted the Red Sea for me to finally go back home after being lost in the wilderness for nineteen years. I was the happiest man on earth that day. Being home with family is the best feeling a person can have. Their love was unconditional, just like the prodigal son's father's love was unconditional. They welcomed me back just as the prodigal's father welcomed him back home and celebrated his return. My friends came to visit me and let me know they had my back and they were there for me. Church members rejoiced that one of the lost sheep was found. I give God all the glory because He did not forget about me in all my mess.

The second event was a Christian youth football camp. This event was the foundation of the ministry that God led me to start. It all started as I was sitting on my parent's porch one day, bored. I was thinking about how there was nothing to do in the community for kids and how not much had changed since God brought me back to Gadsden. I didn't understand why He brought me back to the beginning. God had to chastise me from running in the wilderness from city to city. Now I was sitting still listening to hear his voice. On that particular day, I noticed children playing in the street and a little girl riding her bike. I hadn't done any volunteer work to help anyone since the tornado fundraiser in Hoover. I thought it would be a good idea if I could help kids in my community and bring resources to Gadsden to benefit the city and the kids. Also, to help unite the people in the community for one reason and that was for Jesus. I didn't know where to start. I prayed and asked God to help give me a vision that would glorify His name. Around June God, sent the answer that I had prayed for. The next time I saw some kids playing in front of my parents' home, I walked up to them and started asking them some questions about what there was to do in Gadsden for kids. They all looked at me and said almost simultaneously, "There is nothing to do at all in Gadsden. The Boys & Girls Club at Black Creek is closed." A little girl in the group said, "I heard you used to play football, why don't you play anymore?" I paused and said, "My playing days are over." That's when I saw an opportunity to start the vision God gave me, a Christian youth football camp and to hold a citywide youth event. From there, I went door to door talking to the kids' parents about having something positive for the kids to do in the community. All of the parents said the same thing, "Sir, there is nothing for our kids to do after school or in the summer. They don't have anything to do, and your idea would be great for the kids." When I heard this, I knew what I had to do. I went to see the mayor of Gadsden. He was all in with the idea. Next, I called the Chamber of Commerce and talked with my friend Donna Patterson again. I then called some of my pastor friends and business owners that I knew to get their support. I told each of them I was back home and I wanted to give back to the kids. All of them were excited and commended me for my effort. I had no money so I called people and raised around $1,283 in a week to do the event on Gadsden State Community College's soccer field. The event was a success because God was with me.

I began the Christian Youth Outreach Ministry in Gadsden in 2011. It continued to grow and work well; however, I knew in my heart, God was leading me elsewhere, but at the time I didn't know where.

I was happy at home, seeing my family and friends, so I was content with how everything was going thus far. Little did I know, God had other plans for the ministry and me. I had planned an event, and some of the people who were invited were well-known. For this event, I partnered with the city of Gadsden, Gadsden Board of Education and some local preachers, as I did for all events. For this particular event, I held it at the city's high school, Gadsden City High School. The day of the event someone breached on the contract. I still had some anger issues that God was still delivering me from (which He is still delivering me - it's all part of the process), and boy did I get upset. Coach Perkins was there and saw that I was getting too emotional. When he asked why I was angry, I told him about the breach of the contract and they did not open the guest and visitors' locker room for the coaches. Coach Perkins, in a calm voice, told me not to worry and just move the event to another city. I chose Birmingham because I felt like my spirit was leading me that way and I am glad I made the move. I am thankful to all the city of Gadsden, its leaders, the local pastors, business owners, my family and friends and what they did during that season to assist me with the vision. I am very grateful for their support, prayers, time, and monetary gifts. They helped me jump start the ministry, and for this, I will always be thankful and grateful. It was a hard choice in the beginning; yet, I knew this was where God was leading me.

Today, Above Ground Outreach Ministry, through football camps, helps kids living in poverty-stricken areas in the inner city, regardless of their color or ethnicity. The ministry reaches over 400 young people a year, boys and girls between the ages of 6 and 13. The outreach provides life skills, tools, guidance, parenting, life coaching, and love while spreading the Gospel of Jesus Christ. At our events, we provide breakfast and lunch. A highlight of the day is a musical concert. We teach football drills that are conducted by college and NFL players. They are the coaches who help teach the kids football, and also through football, they teach everyday lessons about life. We have police security, sponsors, and at the end of each session, each child receives a certificate of participation. We make sure the children know there are people who care about them, but most of all, God cares about them.

Giving back not only helped others, but it helped me too and gave me a sense of purpose and happiness. It took my mind off my day-to-day challenges; it still does. It makes me feel empowered and gives me the boldness and confidence to work even harder for the work of the ministry. God gave me the vision to start a Christian youth football camp for kids in 2011. The funny thing about all of this is I didn't have any money to start up the program. I just believed and trusted God and what the Word says I can do and what the Word say I can have. The first year I had 126 kids. The second year it increased to over 200 kids. The third year we had over 200 kids, and the fourth year over 400 kids. The ministry continues to grow because GOD is in it. I learned that it's not about me anymore; it's all about Christ.

I just wanted to do God's will and be obedient this time because my way led me down a destructive path. I wanted to help bring together the community for Jesus because it was needed. Why? I wanted to show people that if God changed me, He could change anyone who believes and trusts Him. With God on our side, all things are possible if we believe. We all need to go back to the home plate and swing the bat for Jesus and then we all can hit a home run for the Kingdom of God! The thing I would tell people is that no matter what we do, God will forgive us if we ask Him, but we have to forgive ourselves in the process. And for the people who hurt us, intentionally or unintentionally, pray and ask God to heal the hurt and pain, while we also pray for those that caused the hurt. Trust and believe that He will answer prayer.

It's rewarding to know that I am making a difference in kids' and other peoples' lives. I have a soft spot in my heart for hurting people and a burning desire to help them overcome difficult challenges, setbacks, or adverse conditions. Even though I am not where I would like to be in my career path yet, I thank God I'm better today than I was yesterday. I learned that God is merciful, and we should obey Him. God was taking me through a process. He showed me that He loved me, and that I was a sinner saved by grace, and He has made me for Himself. Though I have perseverance, it was God who carried me all along. He never left me alone in my mess, but rather saved me for His purpose and plan for my life. God doesn't make any mistakes; people do. I never dreamed that God would give me another chance. It's a wonderful feeling to give back.

Chapter 15
It Was All in God's Plan

There comes a time in everyone's life when he realizes he must make a crucial choice when he comes to a crossroad, that valley of decision that only he, with the help of God, can make. In this place of isolation, pain, and sometimes defeat, we are faced with some of the biggest obstacles that we will ever encounter in our life. We are faced with the good, as well as evil, with doing the right thing, or following the crowd. In this place, however we start, will determine our end. There used to be a program on television, when there were only three channels, ABC, NBC, and CBS. It was called The Wide World of Sports. At the beginning of each program, the announcer said something astute as it relates to sports and athletes: *"The thrill of victory… the agony of defeat… the human drama of athletic competition… welcome to the Wide World of Sports."* When looking at sports from this angle, it sums up what it really is for many athletes, whether they are a pro, semi-pro or just playing the game in the yard for fun…it's the thrill of victory or the agony of defeat. On the field, along with playing the game they love so dearly, there is the human drama of athletic competition. There is the need to be the best, to hear the applause and to receive the accolades, but the number one factor in all of this is to win. There is no second place, and there is no plan "B." That's when it's either the thrill of victory or the agony of defeat. Any athlete will tell you, especially if they are planning a professional career, in sports that in their mind, there can be no other option; there is not a plan "B." They are in it to win it.

Ever since I was a little boy, carrying around a football, all I ever thought about was playing football, and being a professional football player. I didn't have another course of action. I didn't have a plan "B." That was my identity. When all your life, you are only planning for one thing, and something comes along to disrupt it, or it cancels your plans, for many of us, we are lost, and don't know what to do. Your mind was programmed for this dream, or vision, this desire, and nothing else can take that away. It doesn't matter if you are an athlete, a doctor, an actor, or in any profession, when you have to give up that dream or desire, it's one of the worst things that could happen. If you are not careful, you may never bounce back from it because you don't want to let it go.

It's hard letting go of a dream, desire, first love, passion, or a loved one. There is nothing like losing all hope when the dream dies or doesn't come to pass. There's nothing like losing your identity, losing the person who you thought you were destined to be. That's what happened to me. When Curry made the change in position, he took my identity. He took something from me; he took what I thought I was destined to be. I was a running back and that was my identity. That was me. When the position changed as abruptly as it did, I was not prepared. I was lost, and I was damaged. No longer was I the person I perceived myself to be. I was someone else, and to be frank, I didn't know who I was. That was the dark side that no one talks about. I was too young and immature to understand it was only football, and this is what happened in football. However, for me, when the position was changed, it was as if part of me had died. Hope was gone along with my dream and identity. I had an identity crisis. And with my identity crisis, came my bad decisions, and regrets. I wasn't angry at Alabama, only Coach Curry, but in my anger, I hurt everyone else.

Walking Across The Bridge

We all, at one time or another in our lives, have looked in the mirror and saw the person staring back at us, and said this is who I am. This is what I am going to do or be. We can't grasp that the person looking back at us is sometimes saying what you see is not the real you. The real you is waiting for you to see beyond the facade, the pretense, the imagination. It's waiting for you to discover your *"real"* identity. It's waiting for you to let go. It's waiting for you to change. Life is all about changes and letting go, and often with dreams, we have to let them go too, especially if they were not part of God's plans for us. It's all about walking across a bridge. There is a starting point, middle and an end point. We will never know where the end of the bridge will take us, if we never walked on it, or crossed it. Life is a journey within itself. Walking across a bridge is all part of the process, the journey. Many times, we believe we know what to expect at the end of the bridge; yet, many times, when we get to the end, what we thought was there wasn't what we expected or wanted. Instead of a beautiful grassy area with flowers; it's muddy and overcrowded with weeds and insects. Instead of crystal clear water, it's a swamp land. Instead of a scenic path, it's a dirt road.

At the beginning of the bridge, we see what we want to see. We see the dreams and the accomplishments. We see our vision, our wants, and our desires. From our viewpoint, our angle, we don't see the obstacles, the destruction, or the failures. We don't see what's on the other side of the bridge. We are like Dorothy, the Scarecrow, the Tin Man and the Cowardly Lion when they saw the Emerald City. They only saw that it was beautiful. They couldn't wait to get to it; they knew the Wizard would fix everything. They only saw the beauty. They didn't see what they had to do and where they had to travel to get to their destination.

We all have desires and dreams. We are taught early on in our young lives to dream big, and to think big. We are taught to never allow anything to get in the way of our dreams and our desires, not even ourselves. I had only one dream; I had only one desire. The funny thing is that I never saw that in my craziness, my mess, I did fulfill my dreams and my desires. You see, all I ever wanted to do was play for Alabama, and go to the NFL. I did both. I played for Alabama, and I went to the NFL, and also the CFL. In my quest for my dream or desire, I never fully comprehended that I did fulfill my dream and desire. I was too busy focusing on what I didn't get, what I perceived I wanted, that I didn't get a chance to really see it because it wasn't the way I wanted it to play out. I never really appreciated the moment. I was too busy accepting the agony of defeat that I didn't get to play it my way, in my skill set. And sometimes, more often than we care to admit, this is what happens to us. I failed to be grateful for the moment because it didn't happen the way I wanted it, not realizing so many other people would have loved the opportunity that God gave me. In our finite mind, we believe, if it doesn't work out the way we plan, then it's not good, it doesn't have the full effect. So we continue to focus on what didn't happen, instead of what did happen, and we miss so many blessings, because we don't realize that in everything, God is in it, even when we don't see Him, or understand His plan. We fail to comprehend that His plans are not our plans, and His ways are not our ways.

We want the big corporate job that pays well. We want the house in the prominent neighborhood that is in close range of the elite school system. We work hard to achieve these things, and when we do obtain them, we look back and ask, was it worth it? Was it worth the long hours, the marriage, the children going astray, our happiness, and our joy? We want the fame, the fortune, the accolades, and the praise, and some can handle it; whereas, some cannot. Only God knows who can and who cannot. For some, with the fame, fortune, and accolades, they don't let it go to their heads. They maintain stability and humbleness. For others, they may get caught up in drugs, alcohol, and women, which can ultimately lead to losing everything, including their lives. When we first start walking on the bridge, we don't see these things, because from our view, it's beautiful on the other side.

God is such an awesome and loving Father. He keeps us from harm, even when we don't know we are in danger. He sees the end of the bridge; in fact, He sees it before we even think about walking on it. I wanted my will and my plans. However, God had other plans for me. He wanted me to do His will and not my will. There is a scripture in the Bible, Luke 22:42 that reads, *"Saying, Father, if thou be willing, remove this cup from me; nevertheless not my will, but thine, be done."* Jesus was going to the cross, and for a moment, realizing the pain and agony that He would suffer, said, as any human being would, "Father, if there is another way, let's do it, but nevertheless, I want what you want, I want your will not my will. Sometimes the Lord says, "I don't want you to be a doctor; I want you to be a minister." Sometimes God says, "You can be an athlete for a season, but my destiny for you is something greater." How we handle this makes all the difference in our lives. How often we forget that it's never about us; it's always about Him. It's a hard pill to swallow, especially if our plan was all we ever wanted to do. After all, it's our identity. It's what we are known for. When people see us, they see what we do, and we base our opinion of ourselves on what we are, not who we are.

We are more than an athlete, a doctor, a lawyer, an actor, or any other profession we have chosen. These are great career paths, but they don't make up our identity. Our line of work doesn't dictate who we are. They are only a small fraction of our identity and not our entire identity. What happens when we can no longer perform that surgery, or run the ball? Or, how about this, what happens when we get injured on the field, and it's a career ending injury? Do we stop living, and focus on what could have been, the glory days, or do we go on with our lives? Our mind desires what it desires because our eyes only see the beautifully wrapped present; our eyes are transfixed exclusively on our plan. If we are not careful, our perception gets hazy, and we will not see the swamp in the grassy area.

You may ask where I'm going with all of this. Well, I'll tell you. I almost lost everything and some things that I did lose I will never get back. I will never get back those years when I was homeless. I will never get back those family gatherings, or seeing my nieces and nephews grow up to be the fine young ladies and young men that they are. I'll never get those quiet meals at my mother's table, eating her good southern food. I'll never get back the times I could have spent with my father, especially the time before he became ill with cancer (I miss those days a lot.) I cannot focus on those things; they are my past. I made mistakes. I hurt people, and people hurt me. I was selfish at times. However, I cannot focus on those things any longer, I cannot dwell on them. You see, just like football, they don't define me. They don't make up Eugene Jelks, because after everything is said and done, and I mean everything, I am still who God created me to be, in His likeness and image. God has some wonderful plans for my life, just like He does for your life.

People threw stones at me because of my mistake. They turned their backs on me. I found myself isolated. It felt like I was on a deserted island with no one to rescue me from myself. I know what it's like to experience both sides of the world, being semi-famous and then being broke and destitute. It was hard and scary at the same time. Is there anyone without sin? We all have sinned and come short of God's glory. I learned it's a healthy emotion to get angry, but it's not healthy to let it cause me to sin. Don't give other people that power, no matter what. I learned through the grace of God to forgive and move forward in my life. If we don't do this, we will never get to the end of the bridge.

We all have an empty space in our hearts. I've learned that no matter what I try to fill that little room with, to escape the shame the hurt and pain, it will never fill that space. We can try to fill it with alcohol, we can try to fill it with drugs, we can try to fill it with sports, we can try to fill it with a job, we can try to fill it with money, we can try to fill it with sex, we can try to fill it with fame, but that space cannot be filled with any of those things. I found out that I was empty and hungry for God's Love! God has filled that empty space in my heart. That empty space was created in us by God, and only He can fill it. As time went by, the healing took place in my heart. I am a different man today. I am in a good place in my life because I am in a different place mentally and in a different place spiritually. Jesus is the Lord of my life. He is in my life. I look to Him to guide me and direct me every day. With His help and by His grace, I'll make it wherever He is leading me. It's a beautiful thing running touchdowns for Jesus in my new walk with Christ. I realize I am blessed to be walking across the bridge. I won three titles: A high school state championship, an SEC Championship, and a Super Bowl in the Kingdom of God. To sum it all up, God had a greater purpose and plan for my life.

I know now that God was with me all along during my test, trials, during the hurt, and the pain. He kept me from harm and danger on the streets. When I was at the weakest point in my life, it was God who kept me strong. They thought I would crumble, but they were wrong. God kept me! I am alive! I learned a valuable lesson, and that is, sometimes I couldn't trust man, but I can always trust God. I found out that God was taking me through a process of burning away the old man and transforming me into a new man. The old man was bitter, prideful, angry and tormented. The new man is broken, healed and humbled. My desire is to encourage you, to remind you that you can overcome anything and everything with God on your side. He redirected my path and made it straight. He will do the same for you if you allow Him to. That is the kind of God we serve; a God, who is loving, merciful, long-suffering, and gentle.

God is blessing me and doing supernatural things in my life today. He placed me in a healthy place, renewed my hope, enlightened my life, gave me favor with Him and people, restored my family and friends, and opened new doors and new opportunities. I am on the upward path, moving forward and doing His will for my life. This new journey I am on is giving me the opportunity to speak to kids about how they can make it and live their dreams. I feels incredible, and at peace, not perfect, but at peace. I am blessed just being able to serve Him and tell people about the love of God.

When I played football, there were parents, coaches and fans in the stands and on the sidelines. They were not playing in the game. They were there to support us, the players. They cheered for their team and booed the opposing teams. In this regard, there are loved ones rooting for those of us in the game to do our best and go all the way. Life is like a game. Others who have gone on before us are rooting for us to wake up and work, to run with the ball we were given. My father, grandparents and other people I have loved and who have gone on to Heaven, are on the sidelines now cheering me on to do my best and not grow weary and quit. As Jesus said, "We must work the works of Him who sent Me while it is day; night is coming when no one can work." (John 9:4). I have been at the top, and I have been at the bottom of the pit. I'm not alone because the majority of us have been through the same. Therefore, my story is everyone's story – even though your story might not have been made public for the world to see, most of us have something we would never want in the newspapers or broadcast for the world to see. Most of us have something that we are ashamed of and nearly brings us to our knees when we happen to think about it.

You may not have messed up your life as I almost did, or you may have messed up much worse, but you are still in the game of life. You can choose not to focus on the beginning of your bridge, but the end, because it isn't as much how we start out that's so important, but how we end up. Your loved ones are cheering you on, yelling your name and rooting for you to do your best and run toward the rewards waiting for you at the end. Our stadium family in Heaven is encouraging us to be a witness and have something to bring to the table when we stand before the Father one day. We can only play the game while we're in the game. If we are still breathing, we still have another chance. God loves giving second chances. His mercies are new every morning. They are urging all of us to keep going and not quit, which is easy to do when life has hit us in the heart, and the enemy of our souls tries to get us to admit defeat and go home.

The enemy will use his oldest and best tricks against us. He tries to talk us into giving up, using the words and taunts of enemies, or worse, comments from people we know. The betrayals, the hard hits that nearly break us down, which can cause us to curl up and put our hands up over our faces to try to protect ourselves from further damage. We fall for the lies that no one cares about us anymore. The continual barrage of attacks breaks down our defenses, and we just want to go and hide and lick our wounds. The enemy whispers in our ears that they stole our big chance, they robbed us, they hit us below the belt, they took what was ours, they cheated us, they lied about us, they ruined our good name, and it's not fair. Then the opponent tries another tactic by assaulting our mind with memories of our faults and mistakes, things we know we did, detailing them before us. He lines them up like dirty laundry on the clothesline. He shows us every failure and pathetic thing we've ever done or said. Our shortcomings are stacked up and presented to us as proof that we are not worthy. For example, we cheated on that test, we lied about something or other, we stole that money, we didn't treat that person right, we lost our temper, or we hit our friend. If we are foolish and keep listening to the enemy of our souls, he keeps up his presentation and never tires of beating us over the head. He will go so far as to remind us about the time we forgot to tell mama we loved her. Whether it was something we did or something our opponent said we did, there's always hope. We can refuse to listen to his negative whispers and lies that only serve to break us down, or we can listen to the Lord and see in His word that we are who He says we are and get built up.

Jacob deceived his father, but God still used him. Moses killed one of his own men, but God still used him. David had a soldier murdered because he slept with his soldier's wife, and she was pregnant with his baby, but God still used him. Peter, having spent three years with Jesus denied knowing Him three times, and God still used him. No matter what we have done, God can still use us. No one except Jesus is perfect. We all have been hurt and have hurt someone. I made mistakes that I'm sorry for and paid dearly for them. Regret is a hard thing to live with, whether it is the regret for what we did or what was done to us. Even though I have to live with the regrets, I am a thankful man. I am grateful to the Lord for saving my soul and giving me unlimited chances to start fresh in life again. He is the one who gives me my very breath; He is my everything. I am so humble and appreciative of the fact that He didn't give up on me, and now He deems me useful in bringing other people to Him and helping young people in their walk of life; their journey on their bridge.

Today, I am surrounded by positive people; my family, friends and other Christians. I never knew my journey would bring me here, and although I'm far from the end of life, it feels as if I'm just at the beginning of the wonderful things God has planned for me. It's the start of the game, the ball is still in my hand, and now I can run with it because I know He is guiding me and showing me where to run. At the beginning and at the end of the bridge God was with me and by my side and nothing could defeat me. My heart is at peace and singing with joy! I dwell now in safety because He did not leave me in the wilderness to die. My life is safe in His hands.

"It's our choice to build the bridge's foundation...
Only we can walk or cross over our tests and trials in life...
Faith is the bridge standing between us and our
mess while changing it into our message... our destiny." *Gene Jelks*

Closing Words

I am eternally grateful for my father and my mother who gave me what I needed in life. I can't say enough about all the hard work and time my parents took to provide discipline and guidance to my sister Audrey, my brothers Anthony and Dante' and me. Without my father's firm influence and my mother's love for God and her family, I would have never accomplished the things I did in life and in sports, and without their training, I certainly couldn't have recovered from the miserable hell to which I had sunk. I am grateful to all my family, friends and fans for all their love and support. I'm grateful to the entire Bama nation who never stopped loving me, regardless of my mistake. I am eternally grateful to my coaches and everyone who has ever helped me, or encouraged me over the years, thank you all for standing by me. Other sources of gratitude are to my aunts, uncles, cousins, my daughter, Erica, and the love of my life, Regina.

When the enemy of our souls tempts us to become offended, it becomes hard, if not impossible, to do anything but focus on ourselves and protect our vulnerable spots. It is then beyond hope to get concerned about our teammates, or to look at the big picture, what it takes to win. If we keep our eye on Jesus and the goal He has for our lives, and our sole purpose is to win this game of life, then we must persist, push back, stay on the offense, dig deep and fight the good fight of faith. At the same time, we must refuse to listen to the other side boos and condemning chants of the enemy, thereby giving our opponent a foothold in our lives. That's what I did when I believed no one would forgive me and that my life was over. When I turned to God on that cold night under the bridge, I began listening to Him. I chose Him and chose to believe His words and they saved my life. The truth is, we are the deciding factor; we get to choose who we believe in and whose words we listen to. The enemy will tell us it's all over; it's too late, you've gone too far. God will tell us that it's never too late. He will tell us He will give good things to those who ask. He will tell us that all things are possible if we believe. He will tell us that He will forgive us for whatever we've done if we only ask; He will tell us to call on Him. His yoke is easy, and His burden is light. He will tell us that His mercies are new every morning. He will tell us He has given us favor with Himself and with man. He will tell us He has given His angels charge over us, to keep us in all our ways. He will tell us if we choose Him, then nothing can take us out of His hand. He will tell us that whosoever shall call upon His name shall be saved and have life everlasting. So the choice is ours. We decide whose words we believe. It's our ball, and contrary to what the enemy says, it's not over until we win.

Walking Across The Bridge

Life is a bridge. We cross the bridge, but we're always moving, walking, traveling toward the end. As I move toward the end, I crave peace. Peace toward my Creator, God, peace within my heart and soul, peace in this noisy world, peace on my bridge, peace in my relationships, and the peace that passes all understanding. The Bible says, "I will keep him in perfect peace, whose mind is stayed on thee." And as I follow Jesus on my path, my bridge, the most peaceful, kind and loving thing I can do along the way is to follow God's plan for me by helping to point others to Jesus; those who may have lost their way as I once did. He is the Light. My hope and desire for you is that you will allow Jesus, who is the Light, to Light your way as you cross your bridge.

References

[1,2,3] en.wikipedia.org/wiki/Alabama_Crimson_Tide_football

About the Author

Gene Jelks is a native of Gadsden, Alabama. He is a former Alabama Crimson Tide, NFL and CFL football player. He is the founder of Above Ground Outreach Ministry, and through this ministry, he has helped over 1400 children in the Southeast through Christian youth football camps and speaking to them about the gospel of Jesus Christ. He is a Christian motivational speaker and has spoken to various churches, football teams, youth groups and other organizations throughout the South. This year he will be inducted into the Etowah County Sports Hall of Fame. Gene resides in Birmingham, Alabama

www.ingramcontent.com/pod-product-compliance
Lightning Source LLC
Chambersburg PA
CBHW021127300426
44113CB00006B/326